STOP
Assuming!

Bob Schoenberg

Heuristic Books

Saint Charles, Missouri USA

Copyright Notice:

STOP Assuming

Heuristic Books

is an imprint of

Science & Humanities Press

Saint Charles Missouri

636-394-4950

Heuristicbooks.com

Heuristic Books

for Mathematics & Management Science
heuristicbooks.com

STOP Assuming-contents

Acknowledgement

I would like to thank Daniela Malkasian for inspiring me to write this book. At the time, Daniela was a student in my graduate course. It was her Final Project that greatly inspired me to write this book. Thank you Daneila for the excellent work that you and providing me with the inspiration to write this book.

Dedication

In Memory of Sylvia Schoenberg,

My beloved mother

Ch. 1 - Challenging Assumptions Program

Assumptions are thoughts we have that we think are true, but we don't know that they're true. They can have a profound effect upon our lives. What you think, what you say and even what you do can all be greatly influenced by assumptions. What you don't do can also be the result of what you are assuming.

There are two different types of assumptions: general and personal. General assumptions can usually be proven to be true or false and do not directly affect you. Personal assumptions, however, involve you directly and can be more difficult to prove, partly because many personal assumptions are hidden from us – meaning we are not even aware of them.

A general assumption can usually be proven true or false if you're willing to spend a bit of time checking out the assumption. For example, I wake up in the morning and see the sun shining. I assume it's going to be a sunny day without any rain. To determine if this assumption is true or false, I can check the weather. Another example of an assumption is someone tells me that most people on welfare are minorities. This assumption can be determined by doing a little research, such as doing a Google search on a Smartphone or the Internet.

Notice that in both of these examples, I am not directly involved in these assumptions. They are general in nature. However, a personal assumption would involve me directly.

Here's an example of an assumption that is personal. Ben has been struggling all his life to have more money. <u>Ben assumes that he's always going to be lacking money.</u>.But, while Ben assumes this, he doesn't know for certain if this is true.

Sally wants to invest in the stock market, but <u>she assumes it's too complicated for her and she won't understand it.</u> Although Sally is assuming that learning how to invest in the stock market is too complicated for her, she really doesn't know this.

In both these examples, neither person really knows if what they are assuming is true or not. However, their assumptions prevent them from doing what they really want to do. Ben wants to make more money but assumes that this isn't going to happen. Sally wants to invest in the stock market, but assumes it's too complicated for her to learn how to do it.

Most personal assumptions boil down to the phrase, "I can't". For Ben it's "I can't make more money" and for Sally it's "I can't learn how to invest in the stock market. While many personal assumptions are hidden, they are easy to spot if you find yourself thinking or saying, "I can't".

These personal assumptions often stop us from doing whatever it is we want to do. As I said earlier, assumptions greatly influence what we think, say and do. Another way of saying this is assumptions can actually prevent us from doing whatever it is we want to do.

If you find yourself never doing something that you want to do, chances are there's some personal assumption you have that is preventing you from doing it.

Consider some of these goals:

- Losing weight
- Exercising to get in shape
- Starting your own business
- Getting a better job

If you choose any one of the above or select some other goal, ask yourself why you haven't done it yet? Look at the excuses you have. For example, when I ask people who want to start their own business why they don't, I get responses like this:

- I don't have the capital
- I don't know how to market my business
- I have no business experience
- I wouldn't make enough money
- I can't do math

Most of these "reasons" or excuses are assumptions. "I don't have the capital" assumes that you will need large sums of money to get started and further assumes that you won't be able to obtain it. It depends upon the nature of your business. If you do need capital there are various sources to pursue. But most people assume "I need lots of capital and I can't get it.

If you explore any assumption, it usually boils down to the phrase, "I can't". If you've never investigated or pursued such a goal, you might think what you are saying is true, but you don't know if it is true – and that is the definition of an assumption.

I'm going to share with you a three step process for challenging assumptions which is quite simple. Once you learn how to this you can do it yourself.

Step One: Identify your Personal Assumption

Step Two: Use the Special Role Play to challenge your assumption

Step Three: Enrich and strengthen your personal qualities that are weak and those you would like to make stronger.

Each step has sub steps and I'll also include lots of examples so that you'll understand this information and this process quite easily. By identifying and challenging your personal assumptions you can really change your life. It's like opening a door and suddenly seeing all this potential that you have. Many people either have been pursuing something that they want to do for years, but never seem to be successful at it. Other people have wanted to accomplish something but never even pursue it. In both instances, most likely personal assumptions are stopping them.

For many years I've been searching for a process that is simple – one that people can easily learn and then do themselves and one that is effective. I have investigated all sorts of programs over the years. I'd been researching assumptions for quite some time and one day I discovered a way of challenging assumptions. I tried doing it on myself and I was stunned! It worked and it worked very well.

Now, I am offering this information to you. I want to teach you how you can challenge your personal assumptions and unlock your potential. Let me share with you a little story that will make this clearer.

When a wild elephant is caught, it is chained to a metal stake which is anchored in cement. That elephant will try and snap that chain for three days. It will tug and tug and tug and finally after three days it will give up. Then, the chain is replaced by a rope. Now the elephant could easily snap that rope but it assumes it can't. Thus elephant trainers can now lead this beast with just a rope attached to it.

In some ways we are like that elephant. We assume something is true even though we don't know for sure it if is true. However, unlike that elephant, we can challenge the assumption and determine whether or not it is true. This is done using a simple role play where you adopt the opposite point of view and vigorously support that position for a couple of minutes. I'll provide you with all the information you'll need to do this role play and I'll show you how you can do it yourself or with the help of a partner. Then I'll show you how to strengthen any quality that you feel unsure about. You will be amazed at how effective this process is and I'm telling you, the first time I did it on myself I was nearly blown away when I discovered how effective it is.

I will also show you how to easily find these assumptions which are usually hidden and negative in nature. The fact that they are usually negative in nature makes them quite easy to find. Oftentimes there are a bunch of assumptions that revolve around one central one. It really doesn't matter which one you work on first. The process is always the same: 1) identify your personal assumption, 2) challenge it using the Special Role Play and 3) strengthen any qualities you have that you feel are weak. (more about this later).

I hope you share the excitement that I have regarding this process. All of us have tremendous potential but we're often unaware of it and "assume" that "we can't" accomplish what we really want to do. Whatever it is that you want to do, the information is there on how to do it. There are books, cd's, the Internet, MOOCs and all kinds of resources. But, if you assume that you can't do it, then that assumption will continue to run your life. However, when you challenge that assumption, you are released from restrictions like the chains that stopped the elephant. Unlike the elephant, you can challenge your assumptions and harness your real potential. .

I've read too many books that start off with a bang and promise all sorts of things. But I find that many fall short and/or make you read through a lot of chapters to get the nuts and bolts. So, I'm going to present this information to you right away. Later, if you want, you can read about where this information is from and how I've developed and adapted it.

Here are steps to this Program:

1. Identify your assumption

2. Challenge it – using the Special Role Play

3. Enhance your desirable qualities.

Each step will be described in detail and will include examples. You will learn the difference between a general assumption and a personal assumption. This book primarily deals with personal assumptions – how to find them and how to challenge them. As you will learn, personal assumptions are often hidden from us and are sneaky. However, you will learn an easy way to discover your personal assumptions.

Next, you will learn how to challenge your personal assumptions using the Special Role play. After you discover various desirable qualities, you will learn how to acquire and strengthen them.

Additional information about the originals of this Special Role Play and the theoretical framework are provided if you are interested in learning about them

The skills and techniques described in this book are easy to understand and easy to learn. Once you learn them you will be able to use them repeatedly on your own. People report that after challenging their personal assumptions they are able to see many possibilities that they have never seen before. Many people report that it's like opening up a door that you never opened before and seeing all sorts of new possibilities.

Chapter Summary and Key Points

This chapter presented an overview of the **Stop Assuming Program**

Key Points

- An assumption is something you think is true, but don't know if it is true

- There are two types of assumptions: general and personal

- Most personal assumptions boil down to the phrase "I can't"

- The Challenging Assumptions Program consists of three steps:

    1) Identify your assumption

    2) Challenge it – using the Special Role Play

    3) Enhance your desirable qualities

In the next chapter you will learn about the Special Role Play and how to use it. This is the essence of learning how to challenge your assumptions and Stop Assuming. The Special Role Play has an emphasis on "play" and I encourage you to have fun with it.

As you'll discover, the Special Role Play is very brief but very enlightening.

Ch. 2 - The Special Role Play

The Special Role Play is a role play where you adopt an opposing point of view and vigorously support that position for two minutes. To use this role play, choose a personal assumption and support the exact opposite position.

What would someone think, say or do with the opposite viewpoint? Write down all the qualities. If you are working with a partner, your partner can help you by asking questions and even offer suggestions.

Have fun with this role play. Pretend you're an actress or actor and really get into the part. It's only a two minute skit. You can ham it up if you wish but the important thing is to <u>vigorously</u> support the opposing point of view and write down whatever you identify. The qualities and skills you identify will be strengthened and enriched later.

Using the Special Role Play

1. Identify a personal assumption
2. Role play using the opposite point of view
3. Vigorously and passionately support this opposing point of view for 2 minutes
4. write down whatever reasons, thoughts or viewpoints you discover

It is best to do this role play with someone else. However, you can do it by yourself. There are some additional steps that you can do to enhance your experience and they are described later. One of the key questions to ask yourself is: What would someone with the opposite of your assumption think, say or do?

Write down whatever you discover,

The Special Role Play – in Greater Detail

Identify an assumption. Think of something you want to do. Ask yourself, why aren't you doing it?

Usually, you'll eventually find yourself saying, "I can't". For example, "I can't start my own business" Or, "I can't be successful running my own business" Or, "I can't lose weight." Or, "I can't find my soul mate."

If you find yourself saying any of these statements or similar ones – you've identified a personal assumption – something you think is true, but don't really know if it is true.

Is it a general or personal assumption? If you are directly involved, then it is a personal assumption. Example, "I assume that Jamie doesn't like me". This is a personal assumption because it involves you. "I assume Jamie was in bad mood," is a general assumption because it does not involve you.

Do the role play and adopt the opposite viewpoint and vigorously support it. For the assumption, "I assume that Jamie doesn't like me" – change this to "I assume that Jamie does like me". Now, list all the reasons you can think of to support this action. Here are some possibilities:

I assume that Jamie does like me because:

1. She says "hello" to me when she sees me.

2. She listens to me when I talk to her.

3. She smiles when she sees me

4. She acts warm and friendly to me

5. She remembers the things I've discussed with her

6. She hugs me when she sees me

7. She appears pleased to see me.

If Jamie acted differently to me, I would think that she was pre-occupied with something else. I would wait and see how she acts next time I see her. I would give her the benefit of the doubt and suspect that she was just in a bad mood and that I had nothing to do with it.

Here is a different type of personal assumption. "I'm overweight and I've always been overweight. I assume I'm always going to be overweight" The assumption might also be expressed as "I can't lose weight".

For this role play it is helpful to play the role of someone who is fit and trim. Think about what such a person does and how they think. An even better role play would be to role play a person who was overweight and has lost weight and kept it off. A thin and trim person would say:

1. I choose what I eat

2. I choose how much I eat and how often.

3. I really value being thin and in shape so I choose to avoid fattening foods

4. When I'm upset I take action to change my mood without using food to do it.

5. I hang around with people who are thin and trim like myself.

6. I avoid spending much time with people who gorge themselves and are overweight

7. I'm careful what I order when I go out to eat.

8. I avoid "all you can eat" restaurants or places that serve really fattening foods

9. I learned how to change my eating habits.

Note: changing eating habits can be challenging. Yet, people who have lost weight and managed to keep the weight off have changed their eating habits. It's not simply a matter of dieting or exercising.

Here is another assumption – "I'll never change." I've had these assumptions all my life.

For this role play, it is useful to focus on someone who has changed some of their assumptions.

1. I recognize that "'I'll never change' is an assumption"

2. There are things I use to believe that I don't believe anymore.

3. I recognize that assumptions are not necessarily true

4. "Never" is an awfully long time.

5. If I've managed to change other assumptions (and I have), then I can change this one as well

6. I use to believe in Santa Claus, but I don't anymore.

7. I've had other assumptions that I once thought were true and now I realize that they were false.

8. I use to assume that if I worked hard in school, I would get a good job.

9. I use to assume that if I worked hard at work, I would automatically be rewarded.

Some assumptions are more challenging than others. That's why it is a good idea to work with a partner when you do this role play. If you get stuck, your partner can help you. One of the most effective ways to do this role play is for your partner to be you and state your assumption, while you offer questions or suggestions. For the above role play of "I'll never change", your partner would state that and you would ask them questions or offer comments such as

1. Do you agree that assumptions are not necessarily true?

2. Are there things that you once believed that you no longer believe – such as Santa Claus?

3. Are there specific assumptions you once had that you no longer have?

Another variation would be for your partner to ask you questions to "challenge" the assumption.

Although you can do this role play yourself, it is best and it is recommended that you actually role play with another person. Eventually, with practice, you will be able to challenge your personal assumptions yourself. However, it is usually helpful to have another person to help you do the role play.

1. Identify the assumption

2. Determine if it is personally about you or more of a general assumption

3. Use the Special Role Play to "see the other side"

4. Write down all the reasons you can to support this opposing point of view and vigorously and passionately argue the opposite point of view

Here is an example – Running my own business:

- Assumption is – I can't be successful running my own business
- This is a personal assumption, because it is what I think.
- Using the Special Role play – what would a person who is successful say or think about this?
- In order to be successful at running a business, you need to have expertise in a particular field.
- You need to identify your customers – who are they and where are they.
- You need to let them know about your product or service (marketing).
- You must not only believe in your product or service, but also believe in yourself, that you can do this.

Make a list of all these qualities or points:

- have expertise in a particular field.
- know who your customers are and where they are located (demographics)
- know how to market your goods or services
- believe in both your product or service and yourself. Believe that you will be successful
- be determined
- be passionate
- be organized

- be tenacious
- be willing to learn what you don't know
- be excited about what you are doing
- write a plan of how you will run your business
- write a marketing plan
- empathize with your customers

Example – Jack and the Hardware Store

Jack went to a local neighborhood hardware store to buy a part for a washing machine. The clerk standing behind the counter had rather long hair and Jack give him an odd look. Jack kept staring at the guy's long hair and at one point wasn't even paying attention to what the clerk was saying. The clerk showed Jack several different parts and Jack began to assume that the clerk didn't know what he was talking about. Jack finally left the store without buying any part.

Jack thought (assumed), what a poorly managed hardware store this place is. They have people working there who don't know what they are talking about and they don't appreciate well groomed people. Maybe they only like long haired people.

Note that all of these "thoughts" are actually assumptions!

Later, I will show you how to strengthen or enrich these qualities, even if you assess yourself to be very weak in some of these traits/skills.

The Group Role Play

We've gone over a few role plays. Now we're going to do a group role play, where all of you will act as a partner and provide some ideas, suggestions or comments. You could actually do this with a group of friends as long as they understand what their role is. Here is how to do it.

1. One person states their personal assumption

2. Group members volunteer various suggestions, questions or qualities – depending upon the personal assumption stated.

The Special Role Play with a partner.

If you are doing this with a partner, each person would now have an opportunity to use the Special Role play. After everyone has gotten a partner, decide who is going first. The first person will state their assumption and then adopt the opposite viewpoint and provide reasons to support this position. Your partner can help you by asking questions, offering suggestions and providing encouragement by saying such phrases as "what else", "what's another quality", etc.

The idea is to generate a list of several qualities or skills or ideas.

I want to emphasize that this is a Role play and I emphasize the word "play". For two minutes you are an actor or actress. Have fun with this. Get into the role. Once you learn how to do this, you can take any personal assumption and challenge it by doing the Special Role play.

The important thing is to vigorously support the opposing point of view and write down whatever you identify. The qualities and skills you identify will be strengthened and enriched later.

Remember, this is a role "play" and I emphasize the "play" part of it. So, have some fun with this.

16

Chapter Summary and Key Points

This chapter presented an explanation of the Special Role Play and how to do it.

Key Points

- The Special Role Play is the exact opposite of your personal assumption.
- Think about what someone would think, say or do – and you act as that person
- Vigorously support this position for two minutes.
- Make a list of whatever qualities you identify
- Remember to have fun and play. It's a role *play.*

Ch. 3 -
Enhancing Your Positive Qualities

After you've done the Special Role Play, you probably have identified a bunch of qualities and some of them you might feel are rather weak. The following exercises are designed to strengthen those qualities.

Strength Building

Take one quality that you feel very weak about and do the following:

Scan all the times places or ways you've had this quality. By scanning, I mean briefly identify all the times, places or ways you've experienced this particular quality. For example, let's say that one of the qualities you identified from the Special Role Play was being confident. Think of all the times you've felt confident. Think of all the ways you've felt confident. Think of all the places where you've felt confident. Regardless of what you were doing, if you felt confident, write that down. Take a few minutes to do this and be sure to write down every time, place or way you've experienced confidence. You will probably generate a long list. The more you list the better.

Filling in the blanks

Please complete this sentence: "I like how I feel _____ when I _____." If you were doing the "confidence" quality/feeling, you would write, "I like how I feel <u>confident</u> when I (name what you did or where you did it). Example: I like how I feel confident when I work in my garden. (Explanation – I'm confident in my ability to grow a garden. My plants grow good, especially tomatoes).

After you've completed this sentence several times, your sense of whatever quality you are developing should be stronger. However, there are even more things you can do to strengthen one of your qualities.

I Like How I'm ... .

For this exercise, you complete the sentence by using a different quality for each sentence.

Example:

- I like how I'm a confident person.
- I like how I'm passionate
- I like how I'm knowledgeable.

Now it's your turn. For each quality you wish to develop, complete the following sentence.

I like how I'm _____.

Now, if you're ready to go ahead and make this a little more challenging, leave off the first three words of the sentence and just say, "I'm _____". (whatever you want in the blank). Want to make this even more challenging? Say each sentence aloud. Say it aloud to yourself, not to anyone else, just to you. So, while you're in the bathroom and you've got the water running, say each one and even look in the mirror as you do it.

Don't worry if you can't do all this yet. All that is required for this session is that you complete the basic exercise and read silently to yourself each sentence – "I like how I'm _____."

Enhancing Quality Technique

Time, Place or Way you've experienced this quality	Actual Quality
1.	
2.	
3.	
4.	
5.	
6.	
7.	
8.	
9.	
10.	
11.	
12.	

For each activity complete this sentence below. Identify the strength, skill or talent.

1. I like how I'm _____.
   Or, I'm _____.

2. I like how I'm _____.
   Or, I'm _____.

3. I like how I'm _____.
   Or, I'm _____.

4. I like how I'm _____.
   Or, I'm _____.

5. I like how I'm _____.
   Or, I'm _____.

6. I like how I'm _____.
   Or, I'm _____.

7. I like how I'm _____.
   Or, I'm _____.

8. I like how I'm _____.
   Or, I'm _____.

9. I like how I'm _____.
   Or, I'm _____.

10. I like how I'm _____.
    Or, I'm _____.

You can take any quality and strengthen it using any of these techniques. Be aware that some assumptions can be sneaky and make you think that you can't do this. Recognize that this is merely another assumption. It's easy to spot these "hidden" assumptions because they are negative or restrictive in nature. You can take any personal assumption and run it through the Special Role Play and you can strengthen any quality.

Now that you have the essentials on how to do this – how to challenge your personal assumptions and strengthen your qualities, you may wish to learn more about assumptions, the Special Role Play and how I developed this information.

Chapter Summary and Key Points

This chapter presented several activities and exercises to strengthen your positive qualities.

Key Points – Strength Building Techniques

- "I like how I feel _____ when I _____."
- "I Like How I'm ... .
- "I'm ... ."
- Enhancing Quality Technique - List the Time, Place or Way you've experienced this quality. Then identify the actual quality.

Ch. 4 -- More about Assumptions

An assumption is something that we take for granted. It is something that we think is true, but we don't know if it is true. You might ask, "Isn't this true about a lot of things"?" There are a number of scientific theories that have never been proven. A theory, has some strong evidence and is based upon some facts. Most assumptions are simply thoughts or beliefs that we have that have not been proven and oftentimes we don't even have any evidence to support them.

Most people make assumptions and sometimes it is reasonable to make an assumption. For example, it is reasonable to assume that this book will continue to be written in the language that is on this page. Or, if you are watching a DVD that is in English, it is reasonable to assume that the rest of the DVD will also be in English.

However, oftentimes, even assumptions that appear to be reasonable can be false. For example, you wake up in the morning of a beautiful summer day. The sun is shining and there's not a cloud in the sky. You assume it will remain sunny all day. But, just about the time you get out of work that afternoon, clouds seem to appear from nowhere, the sky blackens and a torrential downpour occurs.

The problem with assuming is that we don't know if the assumption is true or false. If you base a decision on an assumption and it proves to be wrong, you could have a problem. In fact, as I've said in my other book, "Assumptions can be costly and dangerous" (Schoenberg. 2007).

Assumptions can be either positive or negative in nature and in their outcome. Let me explain what I mean by this. An assumption can be positive in nature - such as assuming it is going to be a sunny day. However, if it rains and you didn't take an umbrella because you assumed it wouldn't rain, you get wet! This is an example of an assumption that is positive in nature, but the result is negative. It's also possible to have a negative assumption in nature that turns out positive. For example, Helen has to return a dress she bought that doesn't fit her. She assumes the store is going to give her a hassle, because she has lost her sales receipt. Much to her surprise, the store finds her credit card transaction in their computer and issues her a credit on her account. This is an example of a negative assumption in nature that has a positive result.

The problem with assuming anything is that we don't know the outcome. We're only assuming that we do. Assumptions can lead to lots of confusion and problems.

Consider this assumption by Sally, a high school student who always does poorly on math tests. She assumes that she will get a poor grade and is pleasantly surprised that she passed the test. In fact, she got a score of 70 which is much higher than what she assumed she'd get. Her assumption was negative in nature, but the outcome was positive.

Here are some other assumptions:

Jack hires a contractor to remove several large flat stones leading to his front door and have them replaced with a cement walk. Jack assumes that the contractor will put the stones off to the side of the walkway. But when Jack arrives home from work, he discovers the large flat stones are gone. Jack assumed that since the stones were his property, the contactor wouldn't take them. But his assumption proved wrong.

Alice and Craig, who are a married couple are having a house party tonight. Alice leaves each morning to go to work before Craig does. Since Craig usually takes out the garbage, Alice assumed that he would do it on his way out of the house when he goes to work. But Craig was running late for work and forgot to take out the garbage. When they both arrived home, they enter a house stinking of garbage and their guests would be arriving shortly.

Eric and Diane just started dating each other. Eric is a bit shy, and assumed that if he started acting romantic, Diane wouldn't like it. So, he holds back. Meanwhile, Diane assumed that Eric really isn't interested in her because he didn't even give her a good night kiss. The relationship is off to a rocky start because both people are making assumptions.

Assumptions can either be negative or positive and there are four possible results.

1. The assumption is positive and the result is positive. (Example, I assume I will win a contest and I do)

2. The assumption is positive and the result is negative. (Example, I assume I will win a contest and I don't).

3. The assumption is negative and the result is positive. (Example, I assume that I won't win a contest and I do),

4. The assumption is negative and the result is negative. (Example, I assume I will not win a contest and I don't).

The above statements can be expressed symbolically where "A" = assumption and "R" = Result. Plus (+) or minus (-) signs can be used to indicate a plus or minus.

Positive Assumption = Positive Result
$$(+ A = +R)$$

Positive Assumption = Negative Result
$$(+ A = -R)$$

Negative Assumption = Positive Result
$$(-A = +R)$$

Negative Assumption = Negative Result
$$(- A = -R)$$

It is important is to recognize when you are making an assumption. Whether it is positive or negative in nature is secondary to recognizing that you are making an assumption. You are assuming something, rather than basing it on facts. The basic problem with assuming anything is that we simply don't know the outcome. Sometimes it is possible to determine whether what we are assuming is true or not, while other times it isn't feasible to do so. Sometimes, it is impossible.

If you buy a lottery ticket and think that you are going to win, you are making an assumption. You probably can realize that you have no evidence to support the idea that you will win and recognize that you are assuming.

Suppose you park at a parking meter that has only 10 minutes left according to the meter. You don't want to put in any money and assume that you can avoid getting a ticket because you know the meter enforcement person just walked by a few minutes ago. It might be feasible for you to watch this individual and see if she/he returns to a street they have already walked. While this might be feasible, it isn't practical. But you would also be assuming that no police officer would ride by and stop and issue a ticket for over parking at a meter.

Sometimes it is impossible to determine if an assumption is true or not. If you are gambling and assume that you will get a certain number combination, there is no way to determine this for sure. You might assume that you will win. However, until you roll the dice, you won't know. This is an assumption that is impossible to prove true or false until you roll the dice. At that point, if you are wrong, you lose! As I've said before, "assumptions can be dangerous and costly."

Assumptions and Frames of Reference

Oftentimes our frame of reference or perspective influences whether we have a negative or positive assumption in nature. A frame of reference is merely your perspective or viewpoint, based upon your experience. Consider Sally, who had a negative frame of reference regarding math tests. Because she usually does poorly on math tests, she assumed that she would do poorly on this one, too. Due to the fact that one's frame of reference can influence one's assumptions, it is important to recognize your frame of reference and realize that it can significantly influence what you think and do. If you have a particularly strong viewpoint (frame of reference), it is important to recognize this. In fact, a strong viewpoint may help you to identify some of your assumptions.

Consider Jackie who once attended an event where the catering was terrible. She still remembers quite clearly just how awful the food was. The hot food was cold and what was supposed to be cold was warm. In addition, the service was very slow and the food didn't taste good. Just mention that name of this particular caterer and Jackie will tell you –"No Way!" "Don't hire this caterer". She automatically assumes that the meal will be bad if this caterer is used. Yet, the reality of the situation is, if this catering service continued to provide such poor service and food that didn't taste good, they would be out of business. Having said that, it doesn't negate Jackie's experience and it's quite possible that this particular caterer is substandard and may be going out of business.

Nevertheless, you can use strong frames of reference to help you identify whether or not you are making an assumption. Assumptions whether they are good or bad, need to be identified and challenged. Recall that challenging an assumptions means trying to determine whether or not it is true.

Challenging an Assumption

How to challenge an assumption depends upon the type of assumption it is. If you're making an assumption about something that doesn't involve you directly and personally, you need to try and gather some evidence to support your position. For example, you assume a particular stock is going to continue to rise. You might base this assumption on a chart of the stock's performance. Or, perhaps you've read that the company is doing well and the forecast is for continued growth. Okay, you have some evidence, but nothing conclusive. You could continue to research this particular stock and the company it represents. You could ask yourself some questions about the stock and research the answers and eventually, you might come to the conclusion that it is or is not a good investment. This would be much better than merely assuming. However, you are still making an assumption. No one really knows how long a stock will go up or down.

Remember, if the assumption isn't personally about you, you will need to research the assumption. My book, Critical Thinking in Business offers several suggestions on how to do this. The key point to remember is whether or not the assumption pertains directly to you or if it involved something else or someone else. If the assumption pertains directly to you, it is likely to be personal and most likely negative or limiting.

While all assumptions need to be identified and challenged, this book focuses upon personal assumptions and usually they are negative ones. A negative assumption is one that prevents you from doing something or limits you in some way. Such negative assumptions can really raise havoc on goals you would like to accomplish. Some people think of this as a self-fulfilling prophesy. If you assume or think you can't do something, then you are right!

When I was studying Karate, I tried to break a board. I tried it a few times and all I could do was put a slight knuckle dent into the board. Just before I attempted to do this one last time, I told my instruction that I didn't think that I could do this. He looked me right in the eyes and said, "then you won't". That got me angry and it challenged my assumption. I punched the board and it shattered like it was glass. I felt no pain and didn't injure myself at all. In fact, I didn't even have a scratch or scrape on my hand. As long as I assumed that I couldn't break the board, I wasn't able to break the board. Unfortunately, not all assumptions can be broken in this manner.

Consider some of these assumptions:

Leroy is a young black man who belongs to a gym located in a predominately suburban, white neighborhood. One day he arrives at the gym and sees all the bench presses are occupied. He goes over to one and asks a man (who happens to be white), if he would be willing to share the bench with him. The man says, "that's okay, I'm finished" and walks away. Leroy assumes that the man is prejudice and doesn't like black people. What do you think? The fact is, the man really did just complete his workout and headed towards the locker room.

Adelle was shopping for a few items at a convenience store. She brought her items to the checkout counter. The clerk acted in gruff manner to her and tossed the items into a bag and barked out the price to her. Adelle, who has low self esteem, assumed that she did something that upset the clerk.

Dave is a high school student who had a bad day. He raised his hand in a class to answer a question. He got the answer wrong and the whole class laughed at him. Walking home from school that afternoon, he saw

30

some of his classmates across the street. He heard them laughing and assumed that they were laughing at him.

Jill and Tom went out on a date and really enjoyed each other's company. Jill assumed that Tom would call her again. But two days passed and she didn't hear from him. So, she called him, but got his answering service on his cell phone. She made a few more calls but couldn't reach him. Finally, she sent him an email. Still, she got no response. Jill assumed that Tom had just been leading her on and never really had any interested in her. In fact, Tom had been in an automobile accident and was in the hospital and unable to use the phone in his room

Allison is collecting donations for the March of Dimes. She comes to a large house, which is actually a mansion. Allison skipped this house because she assumes that the people are rich and she thinks (assumes) that rich people are greedy, mean spirited and won't give any donation.

Each scenarios described above provides an example of a negative assumption. These are assumptions that limit us in some way or are negative. Notice that they all are personal, especially the first three. Adelle, Dave and Jill all had negative assumptions. Adelle eventually learned that the clerk was not angry at her. He had had a bad interaction with a previous customer, who had given him a really hard time. Dave, later discovered that while his classmates across the street were laughing, but they weren't laughing at him. They were telling jokes to each other and hadn't even noticed Dave across the other side of the street. Jill, after a several days learned that Tom had been in an auto accident and hadn't taken his cell phone with him and had no access to check his email.

Each of these people made an assumption. While they eventually did learn that their assumption was incorrect, frequently, we don't know if our assumptions are true or not. Most of us continue to think that our assumptions are true and oftentimes we're not even aware that we are even making an assumption.

Assumptions that we are not aware of are called *hidden* assumptions. These assumptions are particularly troublesome and can greatly influence our thinking and behavior. Oftentimes we have a vague sense that something is wrong, but we don't know what that is. Usually, we are not even aware that we are making such an assumption. Sometimes, people actually assume that there is something wrong with them. What's wrong is that they are making assumptions and are not even aware that they are doing so!

Oftentimes when we make an assumption, we use the word "think" rather than assume. Other times we don't even use the word "think". We simply express our thought as a fact. Consider these statements which are all assumptions:

1. I don't think the singles dance will be any good. The last one was terrible.

2. I've been poor all my life. I'll never be wealthy.

3. The job interview I had today was probably a waste of time. They will probably hire someone else.

4. I've been divorced two times. There just isn't a match for me.

5. I don't think this business plan will work.

6. None of the weight control programs I've tried have worked. This one won't be any different.

Each of these statements is a negative assumption. Sometimes the word "think" is used rather than "assume". However, an assumption is something you take for granted. It's a situation where you don't know what the outcome will be, but you think that you do. In many instances, when you assume something, you are leaving things to chance and chances are you will be wrong. In other instances, you are thinking or believing that you know what the result will be, when in fact, you don't.

Negative assumptions which personally involve you, restrict your life and deprive you of many opportunities. Whenever you make such an assumption, you deny yourself of even the possibility. The kicker is, usually we are not even aware that we are making such assumptions. **The important thing to remember is that whenever you assume anything, you really don't know what the outcome will be – even though you might think that you do.**

If you are planning a social event, it might be a mistake to think the event will run smoothly or that it won't run smoothly. This is more of a general assumption. However, if you are invited to a social event and you choose not to attend because you assume you won't enjoy it, you are making a personal negative assumption and denying yourself the opportunity of an experience – an experience that you really don't know how it will be.

If you pay attention to what you are saying, you can often identify a general assumption. When you use the phrase, "I think" or "I assume", you are making a general assumption. Our speech is a reflection of our thinking. General assumptions may involve you indirectly, but not personally. The assumption isn't about you, it's about something else. However, personal assumptions do involve you directly and are usually negative or restrictive in nature.

Nearly all assumptions can be identified by asking yourself the following question – "How do I know this is true?" There are several other questions that you could ask to try and determine if what you are thinking (assuming) is true (See Asking Questions)

If the assumption is about you personally, then it is a personal assumption and most likely is negative or restricting. While some are obvious, many of our negative assumptions aren't so obvious to us. Sometimes they are hidden. We have a vague idea that something is preventing us from doing what we want to do, but can't seem to figure out what it is and how to change it. There are three steps to take to challenge or change an assumption.

Step one: identify your assumptions.

Step two : challenge it.

Step three: celebrate your new information and enhance these qualities. I'm going to provide you with detailed step by step instructions on how to do each of these steps.

Identifying Assumptions.

Since the major focus of this book is on personal assumptions, I'm going to show you how to identify your personal assumptions. Identifying your personal assumptions is actually quite easy. Simply think about something you want to do and notice the thoughts you have about why you are not doing it. Consider the following list:

- Starting your own business
- Going back to school to earn a degree
- Losing weight
- Making more money
- Traveling to a foreign country
- Developing a stronger sense of self esteem
- Speaking before a group of people

You could probably add to this list and/or create your own list. This would actually be a good thing for you to do. For now, pick just one thing that you'd like to do and identify some of the reasons why you aren't doing it. For example, maybe you'd like to start your own business. But, your reasons for not doing so include:

- I don't have the money to start my own business
- I can't afford to quit my day job
- It's too risky
- It's too complicated. There is too much red tape you have to go though.
- I'm too old/young to start my own business.

Let's look closely at these "reasons" or excuses for not starting a business. Are they facts or assumptions?

I don't have the money to start my own business. On one level this might seem true. However, there are a couple of assumptions here. One is that you will need a lot of money to start a business. Maybe. It depends on the nature of your business. The second assumption is that you won't be able to get enough money. This also is an assumption. If you're talking about an online business, it doesn't take much money to create a website. In fact, some are actually free! If you're talking about a brick and mortar building, that's a different matter. You can see, that just with this one statement, there are assumptions lurking in the background that need to be identified and later need to be challenged.

I can't afford to quit my day job. The assumption is that you will need to quit your day job. But is this true? Again, it depends upon the nature of the business you want to create.

It's too risky. This also is an assumption. Maybe it is too risky and maybe it isn't. Again, it depends on what type of business you are trying to create.

It's too complicated. This is also an assumption. It may be complicated, depending upon what you want to do. It may not be complicated. The other assumption is that you will not be able to understand the complexity of the situation or the processes involved. This also is an assumption. Some things are truly complex and other times things may seem complicated because of poor instruction and/or a lack of understanding.

I'm too old or I'm too young to start a business. This is an assumption. That fact is there are people both young and old who have started a business. There are some very successful businesses that were started by teenagers. There are also a number of businesses that were started by retired people.

The important point here is that many negative thoughts are assumptions. If you're not pursuing something that you want to do, look for negative thoughts. Those negative thoughts are usually assumptions.

ASSUMPTIONS NEED TO BE IDENTIFIED AND CHALLENGED,

Look at one more example – "I want to go back to school and earn a college degree".

The excuses:

- I'm too old.
- I can't afford it
- I don't remember how to write papers
- I don't have the time to do this.
- *I'm too old.* This is an assumption and there probably are some hidden assumptions connected to this one. For the record, I know of woman who was 66 and completed a Master's Degree program.

I can't afford it – This is an assumption. Until you research the cost and do the math, you won't know that. There are some grants available and there is financial aide. In some high demand professions, the government will actually pay you to go to school.

I don't remember how to write papers. The assumption here is "I can't write papers". The fact is permanent memory isn't lost. Sure, you're probably rusty. But, once you've learned to do something, you don't forget it. Recall is another matter. If you've learned how to do something, with practice it comes back. In addition, most colleges offer tutors or writing advisors at a writing center. Even if you never learned how to write a paper they will help you.

I don't have time to do this. This is an assumption. Are you assuming that you will have to be a full time student? There are thousands of part time students and with courses now being offered online and even on weekends. This provides a lot of flexibility.

As you look over these negative statements, you can see that they are assumptions. They might seem real. Under certain circumstances, they might be true. Frequently, however, negative statements, are assumptions that need to be identified and challenged. Most negative thoughts about ourselves are assumptions. Until you've proven them to be true or false, they remain assumptions and limit what you can and want to do.

A huge part of what we do or don't do is governed by what we think (assume) about ourselves. We place so many restrictions upon ourselves. I can't do this because … and I can't do that because … . But are these thoughts accurate? Are these assumptions really true? Most of the time we don't challenge them. We just keep doing the same things because of what we are assuming. Now here's the kicker. Most of the time we are not even aware that we are making these assumptions and that they are running (or ruining) our lives.

How we acquire these negative thoughts and assumptions is the concern of therapists and counselors. However in this book, we are concerned with identifying assumptions and challenging them. We know that many of our assumptions are the result of our experiences, which create our frames of reference or perspectives. Have a bad experience and you will probably have a negative viewpoint about it. Have a good experience and you will probably have a good viewpoint or perspective about it. But, in either case, one's viewpoint may be feeding an assumption.

Assumptions are sneaky. Oftentimes, we are not aware that we are making assumptions until someone points that out to us. Sometimes, however, we can discover them on our own. As was stated earlier, some assumptions are reasonable to make. But, many assumptions can get us into trouble and can even be costly.

Many a relationship between two people has fallen apart because of assumptions. One person can make an assumption about the other person. Or, both people in a relationship can make an assumption about each other. Even in the most intimate areas of our lives we can and do make assumptions.

Consider one of the most intimate areas of our lives – sexual intimacy. One person assumes that a certain action really turns on their partner. What happens when their partner doesn't get turned on? One partner assumes that he/she did something wrong! To further complicate matters, the person receiving this love-making technique might assume that their partner enjoys doing it, when in fact their partner doesn't really enjoy doing that particular technique.

The assumptions can continue. The next time the couple tries to become intimate, neither partner wants to talk about what happened last time because each partner ASSUMES that such discussion will upset the other partner. So, the intimate encounters become less and less frequent and the couple begins to assume that they have an intimacy problem. But the real problem is making assumptions and failing to communicate with each other because they assume that such a discussion will upset the other person.

In most relationships, assumptions can really raise havoc and lead to real problems unless those assumptions are identified and checked out. In any relationship, there is your perspective about what is happening and your partner's perspective. In addition, you may be assuming something and your partner may be assuming something, too.

The relationship can be casual, professional or personal. Assumptions are not restricted to any particular type of relationship. They can also occur in a new relationship or a long term existing relationship. They can even occur and frequently do occur among strangers.

A young man smiles at a woman who he finds attractive. The woman has just had an unpleasant encounter with a man who was leering at her and began making sexual remarks. She now assumes that this man who just smiled at her is going to do the same thing. He, on the other hand has had a few negative experiences himself with women rejecting him when he asks them to dance or asks them out for a date. His assumption is that this woman will reject him and she confirms his assumption by turning her back on him but not before she shows him a look of disgust. What just happened was an unfortunate turn of events where assumptions took over rational thinking.

What actually happens and how we perceive what happens isn't necessarily the same. Oftentimes an event that occurs is different from how we perceive it. Sometimes we get information that changes our perceptions and even our assumptions. Suppose the young man described in the previous paragraph was informed by a friend of his that the woman he found attractive has just had a bad encounter with another man and assumed that he would act the same. Or, suppose the woman was informed by a friend who tells her the man she just turned her back on is really a very nice guy and her friend knows him. Sometimes we get information that really makes a difference. But oftentimes we are left with our perceptions and assumptions.

The Power of Assumptions

Personal assumptions can be very powerful and maintain a great deal of control over you. Sometimes a person might base their entire life around an assumption. Remember, personal assumptions are often hidden from us – meaning that we are often unaware of them and the influence they have upon us. Consider the following true story. (The names have been changed to protect identities)

When Tom was in junior high school, he fell in love with a girl named Judy. He thought about Judy every day and fantasized about eventually marrying her. Every thing he did that year in school he did so he would impress Judy. He worked extra hard on improving his grades. He tried not to let other things bother him, especially bullying by other students. Ironically, he never really spoke with Judy. But when the ninth grade dance approached, Tom decided to ask Judy to go to the dance with him. He mustered up the courage to call her and asked her to the dance. Judy responded by saying, "I'd love to but I have a baby sitting job". Tom was somewhat disappointed but at least he had asked her out and he accepted that she was busy and couldn't attend the dance.

About a week or so later, Tom heard Daniel talking about going to the dance and said that he was taking

Judy (and he mentioned Judy's last name) – so there was no doubt it was the same girl. Tom became deeply upset. He knew that Daniel was bigger and better looking than him and he assumed that Judy had lied to him and decided to go to the dance with Daniel. None of Tom's relatives, including his mother and father and closest aunt and uncle really believed that Tom was in love with this girl. But he was and he continued to think about her for many years.

Decades went by and eventually Tom met Judy at a high school reunion. He spoke with her briefly and they ended up shaking hands. But Tom still assumed that after all these years, she had lied to him and despite this, he still really liked her.

They both went their separate ways and he never had contact with her again. One day while driving on the highway, Tom was thinking about the Special Role Play and about assumptions and suddenly he realized that all these years he had assumed that Judy had lied to him and that perhaps she really did tell the truth. Tom suddenly realized that he had assumed all these years that she had lied to him, when she had not done so. She was obligated to baby sit, but then the job got cancelled and she was asked to the dance by Daniel. Back then, girls didn't initiate phone calls and she didn't know his number, anyway.

All those years Tom had assumed something that really wasn't true- at least that's what Tom now believes. All those years he harbored mixed feelings (many of which were unpleasant) because of this assumption. How is it possible for one assumption to shape and influence someone's life so profoundly and for so long a period of time? Tom now realizes the power of

42

assumptions and has begun to explore other personal assumptions that are influencing his life.

It should be noted that once a personal assumption becomes entrenched in our thinking, we act in a way to support that assumption – which eventually becomes a belief and often we are unaware of it. This is the amazing thing about assumptions. They can be very powerful and greatly influence us, but often we are unaware of them.

Consider the story of Julio. Julio's parents were immigrants when they came to this country. They worked hard all of their working years but the work that they did never paid much money. All his life growing up, Julio was poor.

Julio developed the assumption - since his parents were poor, he was going to be poor as well. Indeed as an adolescent he was poor compared to his peers. Yet as Julio matured and started working himself, he also couldn't seem to find a decent paying job. Julio assumed that since his parents were poor all their lives, he would be poor just like them.

He carried this assumption with him well into adulthood. Although he had various jobs, none of them paid very well. Julio graduated from college and got a job where he made more money than before college. But, it still was a low paying job. When Julio saw an ad for a good paying job, he wouldn't even apply for it because he assumed that he was destined to be poor and always work at low paying jobs. He also assumed that he would not be hired for a good paying job.

Julio became aware of his assumption and by using the Special Role Play he discovered that he could apply for higher paying jobs and he has the qualifications needed.

Dorothy and Teaching.

Dorothy went to college and majored in Education. She was trained to be a teacher and upon graduating, set out to find a teaching job. She applied for several positions and didn't get hired and often didn't even get an interview.

Determined to stay in the educational field and get a job as a teacher, Dorothy signed up to substitute teach at a local school system. She assumed that since she had trained to be a teacher, that is what she had to do and she also assumed that if she was working as a substitute in a school she'd have a better chance of getting hired. Both of her assumptions eventually proved to be wrong.

She later learned that most schools don't usually hire substitutes and that substitute teaching was quite different than being a regular teacher. But Dorothy continued to assume that she had to be a teacher because that's what she was trained to do. She continued to apply for teaching positions for several years. Meanwhile, she continued to substitute teach and also take on some part time jobs – unrelated to teaching.

So strong was her assumption that she had to pursue a teaching career because that's what she was trained to do that she didn't even consider applying for other types of positions where she could utilize her training and skills in education.

After a few years of substitute teaching she finally started pursing other types of jobs outside of public school teaching. Even though she eventually got a job teaching people how to use computers, she still assumed that she was in the wrong field because she was doing

44

something other than what she was specifically trained to do.

After several years of job-hopping, it finally dawned on her that she didn't have to be a public school teacher as she had trained to be. She finally began pursuing other types of jobs and a different career. But for many years she had been guided by her assumption that she had to be a public school teacher because that's what she had been trained to do.

Personal assumptions can be very powerful. Our entire lives can be based upon a false assumption. Remember that personal assumptions are often negative and restrictive in nature and often we are unaware that we even have such an assumption. Recall that if you find yourself saying, "I can't", you probably are making a personal assumption.

What we are primarily concerned about in this book are personal assumptions – especially personal assumptions that are false. As you have read, assumptions can be very powerful and can exert great influence over us in terms of how we think and how we act. They can exert all sorts of restrictions and limitations in our thinking and our actions.

When we have a negative interaction with another person, oftentimes we think we did something wrong. We might even ask ourselves, "was it me?". Other times we might be able to discern that what happened was the result of an issue the other person had. What's important is to identify an assumption and challenge it. Sometimes you may be able to recognize that you are making an assumption. In some instances you may be able to prove or disprove it by asking yourself some critical thinking questions. These questions will be discussed in a later chapter.

Chapter Summary and Key Points

This chapter emphasized the importance of identifying that you are making an assumption. A general assumption is one that usually can be proven true or false and does not involve you directly. A personal assumption does involve you directly and is usually negative or restrictive in nature.

Key Points

- Assumptions need to be identified and challenged.
- Your frame of reference or perspective can influence your assumption.
- Assumptions can be very powerful and influence your entire live.

The next chapter provides more information about assumptions and has some practice exercises for you to do.

Ch. 5 - Assumptions Part II

An assumption is something taken for granted, meaning that it is something that we think is true, but we don't know if it is true. Most people make assumptions, frequently. Sometimes it's reasonable to assume something. For example it is reasonable to assume that this entire book is written in English since this page is written in English. However, you might assume that this book will be difficult to comprehend, since the author teaches a graduate course in Critical Thinking. However, I think you'll find that assumption to be wrong.

Here's the problem with assuming. When you make an assumption, you don't know whether the assumption is true or not. If you base a decision on an assumption and it proves to be false, you could have a problem. Imagine you are planning a picnic during the summer and you assume that it will be a nice sunny day. Everyone arrives at the picnic and suddenly the sky opens up and a torrential downpour occurs.

Here are some other examples where assumptions prove to be wrong.

Jack hires a contractor to put vinyl siding on the outside walls of this house. Jack *assumes* that the contractor will leave him some extra piece of siding that weren't used. But when Jack arrives home from work, he finds no extra siding. Jack assumed that since he paid for the material, the contractor would not take them. But his assumption proved wrong and the contractor did take the extra materials.

Alice and Craig, are a married couple are having a house party tonight. Since Craig usually takes out the garbage, Alice assumed that he would take it out. But Craig was running late for work and forgot about it. When they both got home, they entered the house which was stinking of garbage and the guests would be arriving soon.

Can you begin to see how assumptions can cause problems? Assumptions can also lead to a great deal of misunderstanding.

Donald and Hope are both making assumptions. Hope stopped by to visit Donald at a time when Donald was quite busy and pre-occupied She assumed that he'd be happy to see her. She became disappointed by his lack of enthusiasm to see her and began to assume that Donald really didn't like her and wasn't interested in seeing her. Donald, who hadn't expected Hope to visit him began to assume that Hope was a demanding person and began to think that perhaps he shouldn't see her anymore. The fact is both people really did like each other and did want to see each other again. But their personal assumptions were interfering with their relationship.

Eric hired a window company to replace his wooden windows. He assumed that the company would leave him the old windows since they were his. But when he arrived home from work he was quite surprised and angry to learn that his wooded windows had been hauled away.

Sometimes it isn't possible to prove an assumption. But many assumptions can be check out. Eric could have checked with the contractor regarding the removal of the old windows..

All of us make assumptions, but critical thinkers identify and challenge assumptions. By identifying an assumption, I mean recognizing it. Challenging an assumption means trying to prove that it is true or false.

Identifying and challenging assumptions is a critical thinking skill. Critical Thinking can be defined simply as a "search for the truth". Even critical thinkers make assumptions but they challenge them by trying to determine whether an assumption is true or false. As you become more skilled you will be able to recognize and challenge assumptions – both yours and those from other people. As I've said, "assumptions can be dangerous" In my book, <u>Critical Thinking in Business</u> (Schoenberg, 2007), I discussed how assumptions can be costly and dangerous. Even in your personal life, assumptions can also be costly and dangerous. They can also be embarrassing as in the example of Donald and Hope, who just started dating each other.

Assumptions can also be a source of distress especially if the assumption is negative.

Sally has invited a couple of friends over for dinner. Both are from coming from out of town and are traveling by car and both are very punctual. When it gets to be five minutes past the hour, Sally starts to wonder where they are. Why are they late? Sally assumes that they're stuck in traffic. But 15 minutes later when they still haven't arrived, Sally begins to assume the worst. She assumes that they must have gotten into a car accident and they must be unconscious. Otherwise, they would have called on their cell phone. Fortunately, Sally's assumption proved wrong. They did get caught in traffic. One of them forgot her cell phone and the other forgot to charge her cell phone. Nevertheless, Sally became greatly distressed because of her negative assumptions,

Do you make negative assumptions? You can reduce and eliminate a lot of problems and stress by refraining from making assumptions. If you do assume something, try and determine whether it is true or not. This is not always possible to do. But, when you make an assumption, you really don't know the outcome even though you might think that you do. You're really leaving things to chance and chances are you could be wrong.

Examples of Assumptions in One's Personal Life:

Sherrie is a flute player and is auditioning to play in an orchestra. Her teacher and her friends have been encouraging her to audition, claiming that she is a very talented musician. Sherrie has prepared three different pieces for the audition.

At the audition, two members of the auditioning committee meet her. They do not engage in any small talk. Instead, they immediately ask her to play. After only a few measures, they stop her. Sherrie is surprised and assumes that they didn't like her playing. They ask her if she has another piece to play. She responds "yes" and they tell her to proceed. Sherrie thinks - "wow, theses guys are really cold". She begins to think that they don't like female flute players

She plays the second piece and this time they let her nearly finish it. Then they tell her to stop before she reaches the end of the piece. Their only comment was "thank you".

50

Sherrie asks, "that's it?". They respond and say "yes" and again thank her. Then they begin writing notes on a paper on their clipboards. Sherrie leaves thinking that they hated her audition and assumes she won't be accepted into the orchestra.

Can you identify any of Sherrie's assumptions? There are several of them.

1. The audition committee people are unfriendly.

2. They didn't like her first selection.

3. They were cold and unfriendly.

4. They don't like female flute players.

She will not be accepted to play in the orchestra. What do you think? What are some of your assumptions?

A few days later, Sherrie receives a letter from the orchestra. She thinks, "Oh no! Here's the rejection letter". Much to her surprise -they accepted her!

Sherrie rethinks about her experience. "Maybe they were just being efficient. After all, there probably were lots of people auditioning. It must be hard to make a decision".

Sherrie made a number of assumptions – both general and personal. Fortunately, she did pass the audition and was invited to play with the orchestra. She was also able to identify and change some of her assumptions based upon her experience. One of her most problematic personal assumptions was, "They don't like female flute players".

The unstated assumption is, "Therefore, they don't like me because I am a female". This is one that

she could have run through the Special Role Play
before she went to the audition.

Mohammed is a young Muslim man from the
Middle East who has experienced some prejudice and
even hatred from other people. He entered a sandwich
shop and placed an order and asked if he could have
the dressing on the side. The man waiting on him
replied, "No!" "You don't like it, get out"! Mohammed
was both shocked and angry and he left the store. He
couldn't believe how rudely he was treated. He
concluded that this guy doesn't like Muslim people.
He also assumes that the manager doesn't like Muslim
people, either.

Later Mohammed talks to several of his friends –
some of who are Muslim and some of them are not.
As soon as they hear about his experience at the
sandwich shop, they all say, "Oh, that guy".
Mohammed says, "yeah, he hates Muslims". But, his
friends say that he's the owner and he acts that way to
everyone. If you don't want it his way, he throws you
out. One of his friends who is not a Muslim says, "he
did the same thing to me". "He has a reputation for
being nasty."

Mohammed asks, "how can this guy stay in
business?". One of his friends replies, "because he has
good food at reasonable prices". "But he himself is
completely unreasonable".

Mohammed still thinks that this guy hates
Muslims, but his friends assure him that he treats
everyone the same way. "He's rude and nasty".
Another one of his friends says, "the guy even berates

his help in front of customers and is always looking for help".

Assumptions can be very powerful. When tied to emotions, they can be even stronger.

In both of these examples, there was an underlying assumption that each person had based upon past negative experiences.. Do you have assumptions based upon a negative experience?

Each of the above statements is a negative assumption. Sometimes the word "think" is used rather than the word "assume". Remember, an assumption is something that you take for granted. It's a situation where you don't know what the outcome will be. In many instances, when you assume something you are leaving things to chance. Changes are, the outcome may not happen the way yu think it will happen.

While assuming is taking things for granted, negative assumptions can really restrict your life and deprive you of many opportunities. When you make a negative assumption, you are denying yourself of even the possibility. The key point to remember is that whenever you assume anything – you don't really know what the outcome will be. If you're invited to a social event and you choose not to attend because you *assume* that you won't enjoy it, you are making a negative assumption and denying yourself the opportunity of the experience – an experience that you really don't know what the outcome will be.

Negative assumptions can really restrict your life by limiting your opportunity to experience life. All assumptions need to be identified and challenged. Many assumptions can easily be identified because your talking will include the word "assume". Our speech is a reflection of how we think. Note also that the word "think" is sometimes a substitute for the word "assume." For example: "I don't think this event will be any good."

"I assume that this event won't be any good."

Another way to identify an assumption besides looking for the word "think" or "assume" is to ask yourself the following question: "Do I know this is true?" If the answer is "no", you are making an assumption.

In the chapter on *Critical Thinking Questions*, I'll provide you with more questions you can ask to not only identify an assumption, but challenge it – determine whether or not it is true.

Here are some exercises to help you identify assumptions.

For each statement below, identify if it is an assumption. If it is, state the assumption. (See appendix A to check your answers).

1) Since you don't like playing chess, you probably won't like playing checkers, either.

2) I'm not an expert, but I don't think your idea will work.

3) Water freezes at 32 degrees F.

4) Since it's freezing in my front hall, it is safe for me to store some frozen food there.

5) I bought a new computer, plugged it in and nothing happened. It didn't even light up. So, the computer is defective.

Identify some assumptions you make in each of the following areas. List at least one or two,

1) Some assumptions I've made about my family and relatives are:

_____

_____

2) Some assumptions I've made among my friends and acquaintances are:

_____

_____

3) Some assumptions I've made concerning a
   purchase are:

   _____

   _____

4) Some assumption I've made about work or
    school are:

   _____

   _____

5) Some assumptions I've made about a
   stranger are:

   _____

   _____

6) Some assumptions I've made regarding
    intimacy are:

   _____

   _____

Assumptions can take place in any area of your
life. The key point to remember is:

Stop Assuming!

Chapter Summary and Key Points

This chapter provided you with opportunities
to identify personal assumptions vs. facts.

Key Points

- Whenever you assume anything – you don't really know what the outcome will be.
- Personal assumptions tend to be negative and/or restricting.
- Assumptions can take place in any area of your life.
- Stop assuming!

The next chapter will provide you with detailed information about the Process of challenging an assumption.

Ch. 6 –
Further Explanation about the Process

The PROCESS – to challenge negative, personal assumptions. Note: This Process is only appropriate for personal assumptions, which are negative or limiting. For general assumptions see the chapter on "Asking Questions".

1. Identify an assumption. Decide if it is a personal or general assumption (If general see "Asking Questions")

2. Use the Special Role Play to "see the other side"and vigorously and passionately support this opposite position for a few minutes.

3. Identify those qualities you already possess and "celebrate" them. Get excited about them. Be passionate

4. Re-evaluate the assumption – determine if it is true or false

Expanded Instructions

1. ID Assumption

2. Use the Special Role Play.

    a) make a list of all the reasons a person with this opposite viewpoint would present

b) vigorously argue for them. Be passionate. Be congruent in voice tone, volume and body posture

c) practice doing this several times and continue to practice each day if necessary

d) strengthen these qualities/reasons by recalling all the times, places ways you have experienced them

For those that don't feel solid or true, precede each statement with the phrase, "I'm in the process of becoming ..." Your brain will recognize this as the truth. Whereas an affirmation isn't always true and your brain will immediately reject it. (this info adapted from Losier's book The Law of Attraction).

Example using the PROCESS

1. Assumption – I'll never be successful running my own business.

2. type of assumption – personal

3. Using the Special Role Play – role play to see the other side. How would someone who is successful think and act? What qualities or actions would this person have.

Here are some examples:

- Expert in specific product or service
- Identifies target audience – knows who are your customers and where they are locate
- Good communicator
- Markets to appropriate audience
- Has a business and marketing plan
- Believes in product or service

- Believes in self
- Is passionate
- Is confident
- Is tenacious
- Determined
- Has drive
- can empathize with customers
- know how to manage fear and rejection

Look over this list and identify those qualities you already have and write them down on paper

- Expert in specific product or service
- good communicator
- believes in product or service
- believes in self
- compassionate, confident, tenacious and determined, has drive
- can emphasize with customers
- can manage fear and rejection

Look at the evidence. Is this assumption accurate? Can you learn what you don't know or develop those skills that are weak? Is this assumption valid? It is FALSE! You can learn who is your target audience and where your customers are located and how to reach them. That becomes part of your marketing plan. You can write a business plan. These are two key components to running a successful business. Have you done this yet?

Example #2 - Ben is bit shy and afraid to ask a woman to dance. He assumes that she will reject him. Using the Special nRole Play – what would someone (Dave) with the opposite viewpoint say?

ASSUMPTION – If I ask this woman to dance, she will reject me.

TYPE of ASSUMPTION - Personal

Using the Special Role Play, Ben identifies these qualities:

- I'm a good dancer. Women like to dance with me.
- I am fun to be with.
- I want to dance, so I'll ask someone to dance
- I am confident about my ability to dance.
- I dance with lots of different women.

After looking over the list, Ben identifies that he actually has all of these qualities except for the last one. Ben now realizes his assumption is false.

Ben decides to challenge another related assumption. If I am rejected I'd feel terrible. What is the opposite view point?

ASSUMPTION: If I get rejected, I'd feel terrible.

TYPE of ASSUMPTION: Personal

What would someone with the opposite point of view say or day if they got rejected?

- I'd be somewhat surprised
- I'd be a bit annoyed or disappointed (Disappointed with her, not with myself because she is passing on an opportunity to have a good time dancing with me.
- I'd immediately look for another partner
- I'd be a bit anxious to find another partner because the music is already playing.

- I'd quickly glance around the room and see who is still available.
- I would ask someone else to dance.

Notice that in the opposite viewpoint – there is no negative assumption and the person does not feel terrible. His focus is on getting another partner to dance with him.

Since this process is a role play, ideally, you should find someone to do this role play with you – such as a friend or significant other. Your role is to take the opposite point of view and identify the thoughts, qualities or actions that a person of the opposite viewpoint would take. There is some flexibility here as noted in the last sentence I mentioned "thoughts", "qualities" or actions. Your partner in this role play can help you to think of more ideas, by encouraging you with such remarks as "what else", "give me another example", etc.

While you might be tempted to ask your partner to contribute, it is best if you do the role play without any contributions from your partner. The reason for this is, if you can identify this different way of thinking, it is far more effective than having someone else tell you. It's kind of like self-discovery. When you discover something yourself, it is far more effective than if someone tells you. So, you should strive to do this role play without specific offerings from your partner. Each time you think of a thought that is opposite of your own, write it down on a piece of paper. You will need this list later.

Going Solo

Although the Special Role Play is a role play, it is possible to do it yourself and a number of people do. A suggestion would be to set a timer for 2 minutes. You don't have to constantly be writing or speaking during this time. But, do strive to write as many thoughts that are opposite of yours within the time limit. After the time is up, read each thought aloud. This is important because it actually helps you to process the thought by reading it aloud. The next step would be "celebrate" each thought. Remember to do this with passion. Add the appropriate voice tone and volume and even posture. If you are saying a word like "confidence" than you should sound confident. If you are saying a word like "excited" than you should sound excited. Practice this several times. You need to do much more than just read a list of thoughts or qualities. Again, I mention both "thoughts" and "qualities", because it will depend upon the nature of your role play and your assumption whether you identify qualities or thoughts. The thoughts may in fact be qualities.

For example, Jennie's assumption is "nobody likes me". She role plays this herself and begins to identify various qualities someone would have if they were liked. Here is what she identifies:

A person who is well liked would have the following traits:

- listen well pay attention to the speaker
- friendly
- kind
- trustworthy

- compliment people genuinely and make them feel good

- honest

- honor commitments

- respectful of people's boundaries and limits

The next step would be for you to personalize all of these qualities that you already have and "celebrate" them. Say them with passion and place the word "I" or "I am" before each quality. You might be wondering what happens if you have very few or any of these qualities. In that case you can enhance your sense of each quality by thinking of a time, place or a way you used this quality. For example, think of all the times or places that you actually listened well and paid attention to the speaker. This is a quality that can be learned and improved with practice. Do the same for each quality. This technique of building each quality is highly effective.

Taking it Further

The next thing that Jennie does is read over her list. Then she reads one item aloud and she practices saying it like she means it and believes it using the proper voice tone and volume. She adjusts her body posture and pulls her shoulders back and sits up in a chair. She then takes this process even further by standing and repeating her statement, paying attention to her voice tone, volume and posture. She stands up straight, standing firming on her feet with her shoulders back. She speaks in a confident voice with proper volume instead of a soft "mousy" voice. She repeats each statement several times. As she does so she begins to feel stronger about each quality that she is talking about aloud.

Jennie now has a solid plan to deal with her feelings of defeat and feeling insecure about her confidence. As she practices this exercise she feels stronger and has more confidence. She now has an antidote to her distressed feelings and as she begins to feel stronger she pursues more of her business activities. Soon she begins to feel really motivated again. She decides to do this exercise each day and then work on her plans to pursue her own online business.

By doing this exercise daily, Jennie is actually creating new neuro-pathways in her brain and she is coupling that with corresponding action. This is really possible to do and it is a practical approach. Notice that she isn't merely saying affirmations. She is only saying what she believes. To help her believe that she has a particular quality, she thinks of all the times places or ways she's actually had that quality, such as being persistent or tenacious. For those qualities she still doesn't quite believe, she adds the phrase, "I'm in the process of ... ". This phrase is one that is taught by Michael Losier in his book <u>The Law of Attraction</u>. Whether or not you believe in the "Law of Attraction" is not the issue here. What is important is to recognize that you can not fool your brain. If you say an affirmation and you really don't believe it, your brain instantly recognizes it as false. This is why I don't recommend saying affirmations. I do recommend doing Validations:, which is a positive statement about yourself, that you know is true. The way you get an validation to feel strong and be true is to identify all the times, places or ways you've ever been this way. (For more information about validations see <u>Designed Change Process</u>).

However, if you precede your statement with the phrase, "I'm in the process of ... ", then your brain recognizes this as true, because it is true. The moment you say this, you ARE in the process of doing it.

The two ways to strengthen any quality that doesn't feel that firm to use is

1. Identify all the times, places or ways you have experience that quality

2. Precede your statement with the phrase, "I'm in the process of ... "

Here is a Summary of what Jennie did. You can do the same thing

1. Identify a personal assumption that is particularly bothersome or troubling

2. Do the special role place

3. Identify all the qualities of a successful business person. (Identify the opposite thoughts of what you are currently experiencing)

4. Write down those thoughts or qualities.

5. For each item in your list, write a sentence beginning with "I am"

6. Read over your list and say each item aloud

7. Say each statement with proper voice tone, volume and posture

8. Use these techniques to strengthen those statements that don't feel true

   a. Identify all the times, places or ways you have experience this quality

   b. Precede your statement with the phrase "I'm in the process of ... "

9. Practice saying these statements aloud each day

10. Practice saying them standing in an upright, erect position with your shoulders back

11. In addition to practicing these statements, do them also when you begin to feel distressed.

12. Recognize that you are changing both your thoughts and behavior. This is exciting!

Beyond the Special Role Play

Jennie wants to launch an online business. She has done the "special role play" and has determined that her assumption that she will fail is ONLY an assumption. She also knows and recognizes the qualities and thoughts of a successful business person. However she feels uncomfortable whenever she thinks about going into business for herself. She recognizes that this is an old pattern of thought and behavior. Whenever she thinks of pursuing a business she experiences the following thoughts:

I don't think I will succeed and make any money. Variations on the theme included:

- I assume I will fail.
- I assume that I can't do this.
- I assume I will continue to feel distressed as I pursue this.
- I assume that I will always be poor.

As soon as she thinks this she feels anxious and defeated. Intellectually, she knows that what she's thinking is an assumption and although she has attempted to go into business for herself before and failed, she realizes that this time it is different. She recognizes that she's much more knowledgeable and this time has someone helping her set up her business – which will be online. She also recognizes that many entrepreneurs experience fear, but they don't let that stop them.

Even though Jennie has done the special role play, she needs to do it again and the assumption about continuing "… to feel distressed as I pursue this", really needs to be challenge.

Jennie does several role plays again and begins to feel more positive and more self assured, but still has this nagging feeling of defeat before she even begins and of anxiety and distress. What's going on here? Jennie really needs to get into the head of someone who is already successful, identify those qualities and develop them for herself.

After doing the special role play several times, she comes up with a list of qualities that a successful business person has. She identifies them as:

- Confident about her service or product
- Tenacious
- Willing to take some calculate risks
- Recognizing and feeling the fear, but taking action anyway (some describe this as courage or being bold)
- Ability to learn whatever skills or knowledge she needs
- Ability and willing to find people to help her succeed
- Excellent writing skills
- Excellent communication skills
- Passionate about her service or products

The next thing Jennie does is to develop these qualities and "celebrate them,

She takes each item in her list and makes a statement beginning with the "I" or "I am".

Here are her statements:

1. I am confident about my service and products. (She really does feel confident about her service and products. She really believes that she can help people).

2. I am tenacious. (She has a slight problem with "owning" this quality, so she thinks about all the situations she's encountered where she has been tenacious. After spending only a few minutes doing this, she now feels that she is tenacious. She is persistent).

3. I am willing to take some calculated risks. (She gulps as she writes this, thinks about it for a few minutes and agrees that she is).

4. I am willing to feel the feeling of fear and take action anyway, despite feeling frightened. (Jennie has some difficulty with this one, so she adds the phrase "I'm in the process of … ".(Losier 2006). This feels true to her and it is true because she really is in the process of feeling the fear and taking action despite feeling scared. Jennie recognizes that she's actually doing this by making this statement).

5. I am able to learn whatever skills or information I need. (Jennie feels okay with this statement).

6. I am able and willing to find people to help me succeed. (Jennie recognizes that she is already doing this)

Jennie continues this process for each item in her list. She recognizes that there are more qualities of successful business people and that she can add to this list and continue with this process.

Taking it Further

The next thing that Jennie does is read over her list. Then she reads one item aloud and she practices saying it like she means it and believes it using the proper voice tone and volume. She adjusts her body posture and pulls her shoulders back and sits up in a chair. She then takes this process even further by standing and repeating her statement, paying attention to her voice tone, volume and posture. She stands up straight, standing firming on her feet with her shoulders back. She speaks in a confident voice with proper volume instead of a soft "mousy" voice. She repeats each statement several times. As she does so she begins to feel stronger about each quality that she is talking about aloud.

Jennie now has a solid plan to deal with her feelings of defeat and feeling insecure about her confidence. As she practices this exercise she feels stronger and has more confidence. She now has an antidote to her distressed feelings and as she begins to feel stronger she pursues more of her business activities. Soon she begins to feel really motivated again. She decides to do this exercise each day and then work on her plans to pursue her own online business.

By doing this exercise daily, Jennie is actually creating new neuro-pathways in her brain and she is coupling that with corresponding action. This is really possible to do and it is a practical approach. Notice that Jennie isn't merely saying affirmations. She is only saying what she believes. To help her believe that she has a particular quality, she thinks of all the times places or ways she's actually had that quality, such as being persistent or tenacious. For those qualities she still doesn't quite believe, she adds the phrase, "I'm in the process of ... ".

If you precede your statement with the phrase, "I'm in the process of ...," your brain recognizes this as true, because it is true. The moment you say this, you ARE in the process of doing it.

Now it's your turn.

1. Identify an assumption you have.

_____

Identify the type of Assumption:

_____

2. Use the Special Role Play and adopt the opposing point of view for a few minutes. Think about what someone would say or do with the opposite viewpoint that you currently have. List all those thoughts or actions. Vigorously and passionately support this opposite point of view.

| |
| |
| |

3. Review your list and say each thought or quality aloud. Celebrate each trait or thought and begin with the phrase "I" or "I am". Say each phrase with passion. Remember to vigorously support this opposite point of view.

4. Celebrate each viewpoint even more by saying it aloud and use appropriate voice tone and volume.

I am
I am
I am
I am
I am

Strengthening Qualities

If you have a quality that doesn't seem that strong to you – strengthen it.

Identify all the **times**, **places** or **ways** you have experienced that quality. For example, one of Jennie's qualities that seemed rather weak to her was,"I am brave". So, Jennie identifies all the times or places or ways that she has been brave. She identifies the time she felt intimidated, but confronted a person, anyway. She remembers the first time she jumped into a pool of water. She felt scared, but she jumped in despite her fear. She recalls the time she had to be assertive with her boyfriend and tell him how she felt about how he was acting towards her and asked him to change. By briefly focusing upon all the time, places or ways she experienced feeling brave, she was able to strengthen her sense of this quality.

Take one of your qualities that feels weak and strengthen it.

Here is a **way** that I experienced this quality

_____

(name the quality) and describe the experience of it.

_____

This is a **time** that I felt this quality – Describe it:

_____

The **place** I felt this quality is

_____

Note: You do not need to use all three strengthening techniques. But provide as many examples as possible.

Still having some difficulty? Begin your statement with the phrase, "I'm in the process of ... . Be sure to say this aloud with proper voice tone volume and posture.

Example: "I'm in the process of" becoming a brave person.

The Strengthening Techniques are not part of the Special Role Play. They are actually part of "Designed Change Process", which is also the name of another book that I wrote.

You may be wondering why I included these techniques with the Special Role Play. I included them to provide you with some ways of dealing with uncomfortable feelings that might arise as you do some of these other exercises. The Special Role Play is a powerful tool. However, thoughts and feelings are usually linked for most people. This is why I included the Strengthening Techniques. If you do the special role play and have identified a number of qualities that are the opposite of the ones you have with your personal assumption, you might have some difficulty "owning" or "celebrating" them. It is important to believe what you discover and feel like it is true. If you are unable to do this, then you need to strengthen each quality as described above. These extra steps and extra exercises are well worth the time and effort to do them.

There are several "self discoveries" you might make after you have done these exercises. You might feel excited about your progress. You might realize that what you have been assuming is false or at least is false in certain situations. You might have discovered that part of your Personal Assumption is valid and other parts of it are not valid. You might feel free and realize that your Personal Assumption is no longer valid. There are other discoveries that you might make.

We've covered a lot of material in this chapter, so be sure to review the Chapter Summary.

- The Special Role Play is a 'special' type of role play where you adopt the opposing point of view and vigorously and passionately support this opposing viewpoint for 2 minutes.
- Write down whatever viewpoints or qualities you discover.
- Examine these opposing viewpoints or qualities and see if they weaken your Personal Assumption.
- Take each quality or viewpoint that you've discovered and precede it with the phrase, "I am" Write this down on a piece of paper.
- Say each quality aloud with proper volume, voice tone and proper posture.

Use the following "Strengthening Techniques" to strengthen your points or qualities, especially if you feel uncomfortable saying them or don't believe what you are saying

1. Identify all the times, places or ways you've experienced this quality.

2. Precede your statement or phrase with, "I'm in the process of …".

- Evaluate your original Personal Assumption and see if it has diminished or no longer seems valid.

Review this chapter and do all the exercises more than once.

Chapter Summary and Key Points

This chapter provided specific information and details about how to challenge assumptions using the Special Role Play and how to strengthen those qualities that you feel are inferior or lacking.

Key Points

- Identify an assumption
- Decide if it is a personal or general assumption (If general see "Asking Questions")
- Use the Special Role Play to "see the other side" and vigorously and passionately support this opposite position for a few minutes.
- Identify those qualities you already possess and "celebrate" them. Get excited about them. Be passionate
- Re-evaluate the assumption – determine if it is true or false.

The next chapter is about Asking Questions and is considered an "advanced technique" because this is not part of the basic set of skills presented thus far.

Ch. 7 -
Advanced Techniques - Asking Questions about General Assumptions

Oftentimes when I'm teaching, someone will ask a question prefaced with the phrase, "this might be a dumb question, ... I tell people that aren't any dumb questions when you don't understand something. In fact, if you don't understand something, it's dumb not to ask a question.

Asking questions is how you get information. There are several different types of questions you can ask.

Questions that:

- • Probe for Reason and Evidence
- • Clarify
- • Challenge Assumptions
- • Identify Frames of Reference
- • Focus on Implications or Consequences
- • Question about questions questions

Questions that Probe for Reason and Evidence

- Can you give me an example?
- How do you know that?
- What makes you think that is true?
- Do you have any evidence or proof?

Clarifying Questions

- What do you mean when you say?
- What's your main point?
- Could you explain that another way?

Questions Regarding Assumptions

- Is that an assumption or a fact?
- What are you assuming?
- How do you know that to be true?

Questions about Frames of Reference

What might someone from a different perspective think?

What might someone who disagrees say?

How might other groups of people respond? What would influence them?

Questions about Questions

- How can we determine this?
- Does this question assume anything?
- The skills that you have learned so far can be enhanced by asking Critical Thinking questions. When challenging an assumption, the following questions are useful:
- Am I assuming? What am I assuming?
- How do I know this is true or not?
- How can I find out if this is true?
- Regarding Frames of Reference or viewpoints:
- Do I have a particular perspective or viewpoint about this?

- How is my frame of reference influencing my decision or thinking?
- Is my perspective valid in this situation
- Am I assuming that my frame of reference is valid in this situation?
- Asking yourself questions can help you clarify a situation. Oftentimes our emotions influence our thinking and cause us to arrive at the wrong conclusion.

Remember the story about Dave, the high school student who thought his classmates who were walking across the street were laughing at him? Dave could have asked himself some questions to clarify his thinking, such as How do I know those students are laughing at me? What evidence do I have to support this idea?

If Dave had asked himself these questions, he might have concluded that there is no real evidence that those students were laughing at him. since they didn't even look at him.

Remember Adelle, the woman who was treated rudely by the checkout clerk? Here are some questions she could have asked:

Am I assuming anything?

How do I know this is true? What evidenced is there to support this idea?

What could be causing the clerk to act so rudely?

Questions for Yourself

By asking yourself questions you can gain clarity and identify if you are using any assumptions or if your frame of reference is influencing your decisions. Among your personal and inter-personal relationships, there are ample opportunities to ask yourself some questions designed to get you to challenge your assumptions

Suppose your had plans to meet with a friend for lunch. You arrive at a restaurant a bit early, because you know your friend is very punctual. You expect your friend to arrive at any moment. But five minutes later your friend still hasn't arrived. At this pint, most people would begin to make assumptions. As was discussed, assumptions lead to either positive or negative thinking. A positive assumption might be, I'll bet my friend is stuck in traffic. A negative assumption might be – *something bad must have happened. Maybe my friend has been in an auto accident.*

At this point, if you are a critical thinker, you will identify that you are making assumptions and you will challenge them. How can you determine if either assumption is true? Call the person with your cell phone. (For the purposes of this scenario, both of you have cell phones). So, you call and your friend answers, somewhat apologetically, saying, "I was just about to call you. I was stuck in traffic. But, I'm free now and will be there in two minutes.

You now see your friend approaching the restaurant.

You might think that this is just common sense – to call. But if you allowed your assumptions to run wild, you could create all sorts of scenarios that could actually cloud your thinking, distort your perceptions and trigger automatic behaviors (Sargent 1984). It's important to ask yourself some questions such as "is my frame of reference (perspective) influencing my decision? Does what I have experienced necessarily mean it will happen again? What is the probability that this will occur again? Is anything different this time or is everything the same?

By asking yourself such questions you can clarify your thinking and make an intelligent decision, rather than an emotional one.

The process of thinking about your thinking is called "metacognition". This is a critical thinking skill in itself. It is not something that one does naturally. "You need to be taught how to do it and it requires some practice. As you begin to use metacognition, you can think about your thinking and identify any assumptions you are making. Having identified some assumptions, you can challenge them by asking some critical thinking questions. You might also identify some frames of reference and see if they are influencing your decisions. Remember that critical thinking is primarily involved in seeking the truth. As you think about your thinking, you may detect some bias on your part. You may recognize that some of your thinking is flawed.

As I've said previously, Metatcognition requires practice. There are many ways to begin thinking about your thinking. An easy way is to recall a recent decision you make. Think about your thinking. Did you assume anything? Was you thinking influenced by your frame of reference? The decisions you recall can be about anything, even decisions you have made about your friends, acquaintances and family. In another chapter, you will get more practice using metacognition.

Questioning Others

You can also use critical thinking questions to help other people gain clarity and provide some reason or evidence for their response or decision. If someone has an opposing point of view, ask them "why do you think that?" Or, "What evidence do you have to support your position?" If someone can't provide any reason, then they are merely expressing their opinion, and unless they have expertise in that topic, their opinion is just that – an opinion.

By asking people questions, the other person can explain their position and both of you can gain some clarity. You may not necessarily agree with the person (and that's fine), but at least you have a better understanding if they are able to provide you with a reason for their thinking. You may have a better understanding of their particular point of view.

Chapter Summary and Key Points

This chapter presented different types of questions you can ask to clarify a situation. Asking yourself questions can help you clarify a situation. Oftentimes our emotions influence our thinking and cause us to arrive at the wrong conclusion.

Key Points

- Asking questions is how you get information. There are several different types of questions you can ask.
- Questions that Probe for Reason and Evidence
- Clarifying Questions
- Questions Regarding Assumptions
- Questions about Frames of Reference
- Questions about Questions

The next chapter explains about Frames of Reference (perspectives) and how they can influence your assumptions.

Ch 8 - Frames of Reference

A frame of reference is a viewpoint or a perspective – a particular way of looking at something, or even someone. Frames of reference can greatly affect your thinking and decisions All of us have frames of references. Even if we encounter a new situation something that we've never experienced before, we have a frame of reference for that as well. Frames of reference can be positive or negative. In either case, they can greatly influence your thinking and they can be tied to an assumption.

Here are some examples:

Jeff once got sick eating at a Vietnam restaurant. Whenever someone suggest they go out to eat at a Vietnam restaurant, Jeff's frame of reference kicks in and he's hesitant. However, Jeff has had numerous positive experiences eating Chinese food. Whenever someone suggest going to a Chinese restaurant Jeff is willing.

Susan has had a bad experience at a large home improvement store. She says the salesperson treated her like an idiot regarding the selection of a power tools. Susan is rather experienced using power tools. Now, whenever she needs a new power tool, she is reluctant to go back to that store because she has a negative frame of reference.

Dan once stayed at a hotel in a small town in the south. He said that the people there were the friendliest, most hospitable people he's ever experienced. Dan has a very positive frame of reference regarding staying at hotels in the south.

Alice is a sophomore in college. She went out with a guy who was in a fraternity. She says he was rude, insensitive and practically tried to rape her. Her frame of reference with fraternity guys is very negative.

Each of these frames of references carries with it a negative or positive association. Oftentimes, there is an assumptions connected with each frame of reference. Alice assumes that all men in fraternities are rude and insensitive. This is based on her frame of reference.

A frame of reference, positive or negative acts as a filter. First there is an event. Then there is one's perceptions of what happened. The frame of reference is either positive or negative. That results in a positive or negative association, which in turn produces a positive or negative association.

(See Model in Appendix A)

MODEL :

EVENT ⇨

⇨Frame of Reference (positive or negative)

⇨results in a positive or negative association.

Continuing with the model even further, the assumption then leads to positive or negative thinking, resulting in positive or negative action.

Looking at the model, you can see how frames of references can influence your thinking – either positively of negatively. There is one more sequence to this Model. – a feedback cycle. After you have taken action, that in turn creates another event and the entire cycle begins again.

Frames of reference can greatly affect your thinking and your actions (behavior). It's important to recognize your frame of reference and realize how it can be influencing your thinking. Then, deal with the assumption.

More About Frames of Reference

There are usually two or more frames of reference. When you read or hear anything, there is your frame of reference and the speaker's or author's frame of reference. When you are reading a book, your frame of reference may be different than that of the author's.

It can be useful to understand another person's perspective, especially when dealing with an adversary. Once you understand an opponent's perspective, you may be able to arrive at a resolution.

Your frame of reference can be influenced and many sales people know how to do this. When you enter a store to buy a a small appliance, you probably have a frame of reference for the price. You may have seen an advertisement or researched the item on the Web. When you arrive at the store, you'll usually see the item you want at that price and other models at different prices. Oftentimes a salesperson will show you a more expensive item. Then you'll be shown a moderately priced item, but usually a bit more than what you had planned to spend. Most people will choose the moderately priced item thinking that the first one was too cheap , while the expensive one was too expensive. So, they choose the moderately priced one that may be more than what you planned to spend.

As I've said before, whether a negative or positive experience, a frame of reference can greatly influence your thinking and behavior. Oftentimes a frame of reference can be tied to an assumption, and that frame of reference can become an assumption. Remember Jeff, who got sick eating at a Vietnamese restaurant? He has a negative frame of reference regarding Vietnamese restaurants. He might assume that all Vietnamese food will make him sick. His frame of reference becomes an assumption.

Dan has a very positive frame of reference about staying in a hotel in the south. He might assume that all southern hotels will be the same. This would be a positive assumption, but still an assumption.

Most of the decisions we make are greatly influenced by our frames of reference. It's easy to be influenced by your frame of reference and to assume that your perspective is applicable in a new situation. But is it? How many times have you made a decision based upon a frame of reference? This isn't' necessarily wrong, but be careful and DON'T ASSUME. One bad meal at a Vietnamese Restaurant doesn't mean that all Vietnamese restaurants are bad. For that matter, it doesn't mean that that particular restaurant is bad, either. However, every meal couldn't be bad or the restaurant wouldn't be in business.

Critical Thinkers are aware of their frames of reference and can identify if they are assuming anything. Critical thinkers also know how to challenge assumptions, by asking question such as *Am I assuming? Is what I'm assuming, true?* (For more information about asking questions, see the chapter on "Critical Thinking Questions").

As you begin to pay more attention to your own perspectives or frames of reference, you will also be able to identify them and any assumptions associated with them. Sometimes it's necessary to change your frame of reference. Situations change and people can change. You might really enjoy doing business with a particular store because they have a salesperson who has been very helpful to you. Your frame of reference may be that this is a great store because of the service you receive.

Then one day, you go to that store and find out that the salesperson you like is no longer there. The new person isn't as friendly or as knowledgeable. However, you might continue to to do business there even though you know things have changed. Is your old frame of reference influencing you?

With a computer, you can update a program. With your frame of reference, it may take several experiences before it is updated. You may need to make a conscious effort to update or change it.

Perspectives of People

Just as your perspectives of a business may change, your perspectives of a person may eventually change as well. For example, Jennie's perspective of Sarah is that she is quiet and reserved, non-assertive and somewhat shy. One day Jennie observes Sarah being assertive and expressing her opinion. Jennie is a bit shocked because this isn't her perspective of Sarah. Something people change just as situations change.

Key Points about Frames of References

- A Frame of Reference is a viewpoint or perspective
- Your Frame of Reference may be different from others

- Frames of Reference act as filters. What happens and what we perceive is happening is not necessarily the same thing.
- We have Frames of Reference for nearly every situation - even for situations that we have never experienced.
- A Frame of Reference can be tied to an association
- Your perspective or viewpoint can greatly influence your thinking and behavior

The Barbeque

A neighbor invites you and several other people to a barbeque. What is your perspective?

A fireman who is there is concerned about safety and the size of the flames.

A vegetarian wonders if there will be any food she can eat.

The children wonder what there is to do while the food is cooking.

Another neighbor who recently attended a barbeque where they ran out of food wonders if this will happen here.

A man who has just exercised at a gym is very hungry. His perspective is "when will the food be ready?"

Each person in attendance has a different perspective or frame of reference. Some of these people may be making assumptions as well.

To Do:

For each item, decide what type or model you would buy and where? Note: if you were to buy something online, name the website.

1) Buying a laptop –

type

_____

Where you would buy it

_____

Your frame of reference:

_____

2) A pair of shoes

type or style

_____

Where you would buy it

_____

Your frame of reference:

_____

3) a pizza

Type

_____

Where you would buy it

_____

Frame of reference:

_____

4) can of interior paint -

brand

_____

Where you would buy it

_____

Frame of reference:

_____

5) Flowers

types of flowers

_____

Where you would buy them

_____

Frame of Reference:

_____

6).A book –

Type

_____

Where you would buy it

_____

How does your frame of reference influence what you buy and where you buy it?

Frame of Reference with People

1) You board a bus and it is raining. Just as you sit down, the person behind you sticks you with their umbrella. What is your frame of reference?

Now – you notice that the person is wearing dark sun glasses . Now what is your frame of reference?

_____

2) You are walking down a street in an unfamiliar part of town. You see a man approaching you with a large stick. Your perspective:

_____

As he gets closer to you, you notice that he is limping. What is your frame of reference now?

_____

3) You see a woman walking who is wearing a ripped clothing. She looks dirty and disheveled. Your perspective?

_____

Later you learn that she had been carjacked, robbed and assaulted. Now what is your perspective?

_____

Notice how frames of reference can greatly influence your thinking and behavior and a Frame of Reference can actually become an assumption. This is why it's important to be able to recognize a Frame of Reference or viewpoint/perspective. A strong frame of reference, whether related to a good or bad experience can become an assumption. Refer to the examples already described in this chapter.

Now it's your turn:

Identify a strong frame of reference you have regarding a product or a store where you bought it.

Have you made any assumptions regarding this product or this store?

Product I bought

_____

Store where I bought it

_____

Have you made any assumptions about this product or this store?

_____

What are your assumptions?

_____

While the above example was more related to a general assumption, Frames of reference can also be applied to Personal Assumptions.

Recall either a really good or really bad experience you had. It can be anything – attending a social event, an appointment with a new doctor or other professional, almost any event.

Identify your Frame of Reference: My Frame of Reference is:

_____

Now, identify any personal assumption connected with this Frame of Reference.

_____

Here is an example. Fred went to a "singles meetup" and had a terrible time. People were unfriendly to him. When he tried to engage people in conversation, they quickly ended the conversation and said, "nice meeting you" and walked away. So, Fred adapted a more passive role and found people were ignoring him. Finally, he felt so rejected that he left.

Now Fred admits he's a bit shy but began thinking (assuming), "I can't converse with people". I'm a terrible conversationalist. No one even wants to talk to me. The more Fred thought about this the stronger his assumption became. Now, all he has to do is even think about talking to people and immediately his Frame of Reference is the "singles meetup" and how rejected he felt.

Fred recognized that his frame of reference had become a trigger to an assumption. He reluctantly did the Special Role Play and discovered a number of times where he did have good conversations with people. Fred also identified a number of traits he has that makes him a good conversationalist. Fred concluded that he can and does converse with people and that he is a good conversationalist because he pays attention to people as they speak. His focus is on them. He is knowledgeable and can talk about a variety of subjects. He makes people feel comfortable when they are talking to him by paying attention to them and letting them know that he is listening by asking pertinent questions.

Fred finally concluded that the "singles meetup" consisted of a bunch of people who were unfriendly and were so fixated upon meeting someone that they didn't take the time to even listen to him and give him a chance.

Chapter Summary and Key Points

This chapter explained that A frame of reference is a perspective or viewpoint that can greatly influence assumptions and decisions. Frames of reference can be positive or negative.

Key Points

- Your Frame of Reference may be different from others

- Frames of Reference act as filters. What happens and what we perceive has happened is not necessarily the same thing.

- We have Frames of Reference for nearly every situation - even for situations that we have never experienced.

- A Frame of Reference can be tied to an association

- Your perspective or viewpoint can greatly influence your thinking and behavior.

The next chapter discusses the origins of the "Special Role Play"

Ch. 9 -The Origins of the Special Role Play -Methodological Believing

Methodological Believing is a special type of role play that was initially created by Peter Elbow, a professor of English at the University of Massachusetts at Amherst. This special role play was originally used by Elbow as a writing technique and was later adapted as a critical thinking technique to help people understand an opposing point of view. In this book I have described how it can also be used to challenge and change a personal assumption.

Initially Professor Elbow told his students,, "If a reader responds to your writing by saying something that seems wrong, don't disagree, don't argue, just listen and try to see your text through that reader's eyes". (Elbow. <u>Writing Without Teachers</u>). Professor Elbow created what he called the "Believing Game", where we are "... not just listening to views different from our own and holding back from arguing with them ... but actually *trying* to believe them" (Elbow 2009). He also stated that "It's not natural to try to believe ideas we disagree with or even hate."

In my online graduate course offered via the University of Massachusetts at Boston, I have been teaching my students Methodological Believing for several years. Clearly, this is a skill that requires practice. However, I can assure you, it is well worth taking the time to practice. Even in the Believing Game, Professor Elbow talks about assumptions as he states, "The flaws in our own thinking usually come from our assumptions---our ways of thinking that we accept without noticing--assumptions that are part of the very *structure of* our thinking." (2009, pg 7).

In talking about the Believing Game, Elbow states, "Give me the view in your head. You are having an experience I don't have: help me to have it. "

(Elbow 1986 pg 261 (Embracing Contraries)

To help people believe, Elbow suggests that individuals answer the following questions:

What's interesting or helpful about this view? What are some intriguing features that others might not have noticed? What would you notice if you believed this view? If it were true? In what sense or under what conditions might this idea be true? (Elbow 1986 pg 275)

The way the Believing Game is used in Critical Thinking is to vigorously support an opposing point of view – a view that is opposite of your view. Elbow suggested doing this for five minutes and I have since adopted a "two minute rule". This two minute rule is used in a special role play which is known as Methodological Believing. (For our purposes, we will only do this Special Role Play for 2 minutes. During that time, you adopt an opposing point of view and vigorously and passionately support that position and write down whatever thoughts or ideas that you have).

Although Elbow created the Believing Game for a writing class, it has since been adapted as a Critical Thinking Skill. Much more recently, one of my graduate students used it as a way of getting one of her visually impaired student to look at her assumptions.

Initially, one of my graduate students was wondering what to do for a Final Project – a requirement of the Critical Thinking Course, which I teach online via the University of Massachusetts at Boston. After she described her job to me, which was teaching visually impaired students, she told me that many visually impaired students make and live with lots of assumptions. She described one student in particular who was making several assumptions in her personal life that were really quite limiting and negatively impacting upon her quality of life. (More details are provided in the next chapter)

For my graduate student's Final Project, in consultation with me, she decided to teach her student about assumptions and play the Believing Game with her. In essence, what she was going to do was role play with her and help her examine her assumptions. Her Project was highly successful and inspired me to write this book. On the following pages, you can read about her Project.

In essence Methodological Believing is a special role play where you vigorously support an opposing point of view for a brief period of time. More recently, I have adapted this role play for people to examine their personal assumptions and focus on the exact opposite viewpoint of whatever their assumptions may be. I have personally used this technique on myself with surprisingly positive results.

Although I have provided lots of details about Methodological Believing, it is essentially a special role play that can be reduced to the following steps:

1. identify a personal assumption

2. role play using the opposite point of view

2. vigorously and passionately support this opposing point of view for 2 – 5 minutes

3. write down whatever reasons, thoughts or viewpoints you discover

It is best to do this role play with someone else. However, you can do it by yourself. There are some additional steps that you can do to enhance your experience and they are described later. One of the key questions to ask yourself is, "How would someone with the opposite assumption of what you have, act or do? What would this person say?

The Special Role Play was further adapted by Daniela Malkasian, who was a graduate student of mine. Daniela did a Class Project (as part of the requirements for completion of her course with me) where she used the Special Role Play to help one of her blind students identify her assumptions and frames of references that were having a very restrictive and negative effect upon this student's life.

Here is a portion of her Project. (The author of this book gratefully acknowledges the influence Danielle Malkasian's work had upon the inspiration to write this book).

"Assumptions and Frames of Reference in a Legally Blind Student"

"Individuals with visual impairments or legal blindness tend to have misconceptions of the world around them", according to Malkasian (2014). They are often faced with feeling different from other people. In her paper, DM focuses on the concepts of identifying and challenging assumptions, and identifying frames of reference (perspective).. These concepts were taught and applied to a legally blind high school student through various activities involving the special role play and answering some critical thinking questions... .

The purpose of this process was to help the student learn and apply critical thinking skills (such as challenging assumptions) in her everyday life (specifically in a social setting with the hope and expectation that she will develop a more) profound perspective of the world around her (Malkasian 2014).

The Special Role Play took place during several one hour sessions in a room at the high school. The student and instructor created three social settings that the student wanted to discuss and used the Special Role Play. These concepts were selected randomly by writing them on pieced of paper and placing them in a hat. The student selected a situation from the hat and that topic was discussed in terms of assumptions, frames of reference, and the Special Role Play. Once this was completed, the student was asked to apply what was talked about into their daily experiences during the school day. At the end of the week the student and the Instructor discussed the observations that were made regarding assumptions and frames of references that were challenged, and any other forms of critical thinking that took place (Malkasian 2014)

Overview

Using the information the Instructor (who was in my graduate course at the time) had learned during the semester, she created an activity to use with her high school student who is legally blind. This game focused on a role play which became the "Special Role Play" to help the student challenge her assumptions. The game created an environment where the student was asked to challenge her assumptions and frames of reference that she had. This student in particular was described by DM as being very naïve and sheltered. "In her culture, women and girls are to stay in the house to cook, clean, and serve the men; getting an education and voicing their opinion is simply frowned upon" (DM). Given that her student was already at a disadvantage of being legally blind, there were instances where she did not understand "… social norms,

100

emotions, and how to react or interact with a peer in a social setting. (Malkasian 2014)) The game that Malkasian created can be changed to accommodate any age group of students "… with or without visual impairments" According to Malkasian, "It is a game that tests the student's methodological thinking and assumptions that they have derived from experiences (2014) [Author's note: "Methodological thinking was the original name for this role play. I renamed it the "Special Role Play"].

Format

The following information is directly from DM's paper. Words in italics are her actual words.

- This activity will take place over the course of several weeks
- The student and teacher will come up with 3 social interactions or situations that the student has faced or think they will face in the future.
- The situation will be written on a piece of paper and placed into a hat or bucket.
- The student will pick a topic out of the hat. The student will not move on to a new topic until they feel that they have mastered a clear understanding of what assumptions and frames of reference have been challenged (one topic for each week is the goal).
- Once the student is able to identify these key components, they will come up with alternative ways to look at the situation at hand and apply their new perspective in and out of the classroom
- The student will then report on their findings, how they felt, and what changes, if any, they would make.

Situation 1

Topic: In the first situation the student described that sometimes other students walk in to the room and say "hello" to her and she doesn't know who they are.

Discussion Question: "What could you do so that you may know who it is that is saying hello to you?") DM

Role Playing

What follows is a transcript of the actual conversation that took place between the Teacher and her Student. I have placed all conversation I italics.

Teacher: *Let's pretend that you are the "stranger" and I am you.*

Student: *Okay.*

Teacher: *Okay, imagine that I am walking down the hallway and you see me. We are in front of each other what do you do or say?*

Student: *"Hi _____! How are you?"*

Teacher: *"Hi... I am not sure I recognize your voice. Could you tell me who you are?"*

Student: Wait, Mrs. M... wouldn't that make the other person saying hi uncomfortable and not want to say hi again? I don't want to hurt their feelings because I don't recognize their voice. I don't want people to think that I am mean or don't remember them.

Teacher: *Well, let's put yourself in their shoes. Do you think you would feel hurt because someone who cannot see is asking for you to identify yourself?*

Student: *Well I guess not. They can't see so how are they supposed to know who you are, right?*

Teacher: *Right, it could also be a safety issue – trying to see if the person who is talking to them is someone that they know or a stranger they have never spoken to. If this is a stranger they have never encountered then they may feel unsafe and decide to leave to a safe area.*

Student: *I never thought of it that way. I just always say "hi" back to the person because I don't want them to be upset with me. I guess I should try to ask more questions even if it can be uncomfortable.*

Application: Challenging assumptions

Author's note: In the above dialogue, the student was able to identify her assumption that she assumed people would be upset with her if she asked who they were. Consequently, she hadn't asked who they were and didn't always recognize their voices.

(Author's Note: In this next section. another one of this student's assumption is challenged.

Situation 2

Topic: How do I know if someone is being kind to me or just feels bad for me because I am blind?

Discussion Question: Why do you feel this way? Is there a reason that you would believe or assume that any individual is just being kind to you because you are blind? How can we change this belief?

The student and I have a very close relationship. She has opened up to me as an "older sister" but still respecting me as her teacher. She has a difficult time building trust with those around her, so when she is able to express herself to me I know that it is a big step for her (DM)

Role Playing

This is an actual transcript. The conversation is in italics.

Teacher: *(Students name)! Hi! During math today do you want me to sit next to you and tell you what's going on?? I can help you on your whiteboard or record the notes for you??*

Student: *Hi….you don't have to…I can just ask my para to do it.*

Teacher: *Are you sure? I don't mind! I like helping.*

Student: *…. yes. Thanks though.*

Teacher: *(Student's name), tell me why you answered the way you did to this person who wants to help?*

Student: *I don't know. It just seems weird. Who gets excited to help someone who is blind? What if they are just saying it so it makes them look good? I don't trust people you know this.*

Teacher: *I understand that you have a difficult time trusting people, but I want you to remember that there are adults in the classroom, including your para who always sits near you. I am sure if this student was not being genuine or truly helping you your para would step in.*

Student: *Yeah … I guess you're right. Maybe not everyone is mean and feels bad for me. But I am sure some people do! And you can't tell me I am wrong!*

Teacher: *Well, you are entitled to your opinion as an adult. I personally do not think that in this situation the student was just being nice to you because you are blind. I think they wanted to help you learn and received all of the information that is being presented in class. Sometimes you miss some of the lesson because materials are being enlarged for you, or because it takes you a little longer to understand what is happening in the lesson. I think this was a very kind and genuine gesture.*

Student: *So next time someone asks to help me I shouldn't hesitate and say no? I should try to say yes.... I guess I can start to try doing that. No promises, but I will try.*

Teacher: *All I want you to do is try. It is not going to happen overnight, but eventually you will find it easier to ask and receive help with lots of practice.*

Student: *I know. I really should start listening to you more often...you are older and wiser (student laughs and smiles)*

Teacher: *I am here to help!*

Application: Frame of reference and assumptions challenged.

Conclusion

Author's Note: Shortly after doing these special role plays with her teacher, the student volunteered to work with other students and designed her own questions and led discussions.

"This shift in confidence and ability to express her emotions is wonderful. It has shown me that with some small discussions, evaluating why situations occurred, how to change the outcome, and where our belief has stemmed from can make a world of difference in someone's life that has such limited exposure to society" (Malkasian 2014).

Frames of Reference simply means one's perspective or point of view. The Special Role play was adapted from Peter Elbow's Methodological Believing technique. These skills and techniques are critical thinking skills. Critical Thinking is a term with hundreds of definitions. I like to define it as "a search for the truth"

Author's note: Danielle Malkasian's work had a profound effect upon her blind student. This student, who initially lived a very sheltered life and was introverted, completely changed. She actually volunteered to run these special sessions that her teacher had initially created for her. She became a "normal" teenager in terms of being legally blind and socializing and participating in a variety of social activities. Her progress inspired me so much, that I decided to write this book and teach people how to identify and challenge their assumptions. It is a rare event to actually see the results of my own teaching being put into practice. Daniela had extraordinary results with her student and went on to teach other students as well. I am so pleased that what began as a discussion about an academic requirement for the course resulted in such a profound change for her student. If a legally blind high school student can make such a profound change in her life, imagine what YOU can do!

Ch, 10 -
What the Special Role Play Does

When you use the Special Role Play several things
happen:

1. **You are countering an existing thought or belief**.

    When you use the Special Role Play you are
    countering an existing thought or belief. The very
    nature of the Special Role Play allows you to
    "play" and adapt a role and consider possibilities
    that you would not ordinarily consider. The
    Special Role Play allows you to be flexible and
    actually step out of the rigid, restrictive ways of
    thinking that you may be engaging without even
    being aware of it.

In the Designed Change Process Model of Behavior
(Schoenberg 2013), there are two different types of
behavior described. One is Automatic and rigid with
very little awareness, while the other is Intentional with
flexibility and a maximum amount of choice. Because
the Special Role Play is designed to be "playful", it
allows you to step out of the rigid way of thinking and
discovered new possibilities. You discover on your own,
several possibilities that you probably never really
considered before. While other people can probably see
these traits and characteristics, it is much more effective
if you discover them yourself through the role play. The
fact that you may not believe you actually possess these
qualities is addressed with the Enhancement techniques.

2. **You are developing alternatives to your assumed thought or belief..**

By engaging in the Special Role Play, you are actually developing alternatives to your assumed thought or belief. Again, many of these alternatives will be developed with the Enhancement techniques. Often, the mere act of identifying some new possibilities is an action in itself. Remember, you are in a role for a very limited period of time. Even a couple of minutes can be very beneficial. The mere act of thinking of a different possibility actually begins to create an alternative to your assumption as you begin to realize that maybe what you've been assuming may be untrue or is only true in certain situations or circumstance.

3. **You are building the foundation for a new behavior.**

As you discover your new traits and characteristics, you are building the foundation for a new behavior. While this requires practice, awareness is the first step. By discovering alternatives and "enhancing" those alternatives, you are actually engaging in Intentional Behavior (Schoenberg 2013), which is not possible to do while you are assuming. Another way of explaining this is – if you are in Automatic Behavior, you will not have the flexibility and awareness of other possibilities.

4. **You are beginning to rewire your brain.**

Neuroscientists have proven that if you practice a new behavior, you can create a new neuro-pathway in your brain. While this takes practice with lots of repetition, it is only possible to do if you have the awareness and are open to the possibility that maybe what you've been assuming is untrue.

108

By engaging in the Special Role Play you will open the door to all sorts of possibilities that previously were hidden from you. People often describe this experience as suddenly having a door open which leads to all sorts of possibilities they never considered before. In essence, you are developing a self administered skill that enables you to change your thinking and behavior. What allows you to step into Intentional Behavior is the playfulness of this role "play".

What Self Enhancement Does

1. It strengthens various desirable qualities and traits

2. It increase Emotional Intelligence. (This is an entire topic in itself. Basically the enhancement techniques allow you to remain in a positive emotional state.

3. It strengthens your self esteem and a sense of your abilities

4. It provides access to Intentional Behavior (see Designed Change Process)

5. It reduces stress and promotes an overall sense of please with oneself.

While it is important for you to understand how to do the Special Role Play, it is not important for you to understand the theoretical framework behind it. The important thing is to be able to do the Special Role play to challenge you assumptions. The terms "Automatic Behavior" and "Intentional Behavior are part of a model of behavior described in the Designed Change Process. If you are interested in learning more about his, you may wish to read my book entitled, <u>Designed Change Process</u> (Schoenberg 2013).

Once you have done the Special Role Play, you can enhance each trait or quality by doing the Enhancement techniques. These techniques help you to strengthen each desirable quality. Again, it is unnecessarily for you to understand the theoretical framework behind each skill/technique. What is important is that you understand how to do them and that you actually do them.

In summary, the Special Role Play and the Enhancement techniques offer simple, yet powerful ways of making positive changes in your life by challenging your personal assumptions and enhancing desirable positive qualities. . Here are the steps:

1. Identify an assumption and determine whether it is general or personal

2. Do the Special Role Play and identify various qualities/skills that you desire

3. Use the Enhancement techniques to strengthen these desirable qualities.

Ch 11 Technical Framework

This chapter is somewhat technical and provides a theoretical framework for people who want a technical explanation as to how this Process works. If you're only interested in the practical application, you can skip this chapter.

The Stop Assuming program is based upon Critical Thinking Skills and principles. Critical Thinking is an interdisciplinary field involving Education, Philosophy and Psychology. While the term "critical thinking" has hundreds of definitions, essentially critical thinking involves a 'search for the truth'.

The following critical thinking skills are used in the Program and will be discussed in detail: Identifying and Challenging Assumptions, Methodological Believing , Frames of Reference and Metacognition

Identifying and Challenging Assumptions

This skill is self explanatory except "challenging" means to determine if the assumption is true or not. In this book we are primarily concerned with Personal Assumptions which have been described as *negative* or *restrictive* in nature. Although Personal Assumptions can be rather sneaky and we are often unaware of them, they are easy to find. Whenever you want to do something but "can't", chances are there is a personal assumption involved. To find these personal assumptions, merely ask yourself "why can't I"? You will easily identify several reason or excuses why you can't do whatever it is that you want to do. These "reasons" are most likely personal assumptions. Recall that an assumption is something you think is true but don't know if it really is true. A significant portion of this Program is the ability to recognize Personal Assumptions and challenge them.

Methodological Believing

The "Special Role Play" is an adaptation of Methodological Believing. Originally created by Professor Peter Elbow, an English professor at UMASS at Amherst, the skill was used to help students understand an opposing point of view. It was later accepted and developed as a critical thinking skill by the Critical & Creative Thinking Program at UMASS, Boston. Essentially, this was a role play to help you understand an opposing point of view. I modified and adapted this skill for use in this book after a graduate student of mine used it to help a legally blind student identify and challenge some of her assumptions. The actual skill and instructions on how to do it are provided in great detail in earlier chapters in this book.

Frames of Reference

This is another critical Thinking skill which simply means a perspective or viewpoint. While in the broader field of Critical Thinking, this skill involves identifying various frames of reference (perspectives), for our purposes we are primarily concerned with identifying our own perspective or viewpoint. There can be a relationship between one's frame of reference and one's assumption(s). For example, if I have a particularly good or bad experience with a product or a store, I might begin to assume that it will always be that way. Since we are primarily concerned with Personal Assumptions, consider the following: Alice who is single went to a Single's Dance. She had a miserable time because no one asked her to dance. He frame of reference or viewpoint about Single's Dances is very negative. Consequently she assumes that all single's dances are going to be bad – so she avoids them. Her Frame of Reference has become a Personal Assumption. This assumption steers Alice away from future single's dances. She may even begin to associate other types of singles events to be the same as single's dances. Eventually Alice might even develop a much broader assumption that <u>all</u> single's events are no good. If you were to ask Alice why she doesn't go to single's events she might say something like, "I can't". I have such a miserable time when I go to them. But, Alice is making an assumption. She doesn't really know if all single's events are bad. She might go to one and meet the man of her dreams. But, because she assumes she will have a miserable time, she doesn't go to any. Her personal assumption is both negative and restricting.

Metacognition

Metacogntion means "thinking about one's thinking". This is not something that one usually does unless one is taught how to do it. It is an extremely important critical thinking skill because it often involves using several other critical thinking skills. Using Metacogniton, I might check to see if I am making any assumptions. I think about my thinking and ask myself the question – "Am I making any assumptions" or Am I assuming something" I might also examine my frames of reference and see if they are influencing me in either a positive or negative way. I might even look to see if my frame of reference has become an assumption and further challenge that assumption by using Methodologcial Believing or as we call it in this book, the "Special Role Play".

Enhancement Techniques

The Enhancement Techniques which will be described below are from the Designed Change Process (Schoenberg 2013). These are various activities and exercises that strengthen (enhance) various personal traits and qualities that you might feel are weak or even non-existent.. These techniques have been adapted for use in this Program. The actual techniques involved are enjoyable activities "I like how I'm_____." and "I'm ___, They are part of the Designed Change Process, and are referred to as "Validation Techniques, designed to strengthen personal qualities and enhance one's sense of self esteem. The Design Change Process was created by Tom Sargent. What follows is a discussion of each technique

THE TECHNIQUES

I like how I feel _____ when I _____. In the first blank you identify a specific feeling and in the second blank you identify the activity you do when you get that feeling. Example, I like I how feel relaxed when I work in my garden. Or, "I like how I feel joyous when I'm dancing".

If may be easier to reverse the order of this exercise as follows: "When I _____ I feel _____. It is easy to identify something that you like to do. However, it can be a bit more challenging to identify the feeling you get from doing that activity. This happens because most of the time we simply express how we feel as either "good" or "bad". Usually, we have many more descriptions of what "bad" feel like than what "good" feels like.

"I like how I'm _____. This is actually part of the Enhancing Quality Technique. Using this technique, you identify the specific quality you have. This could be a strength, skill or talent. For example, if one of your enjoyable activities is dancing, you would identify various skills, strengths or talents you use to dance, such as being coordinated, having a good sense of rhythm, ability to remember steps, etc. Using this technique you would fill in the blank by saying/writing – "I like how I'm coordinated", or "I like how I have a good sense of rhythm" or "I like how I remember dance steps". In essence, what you are doing when you use this technique is focusing upon a specific strength, skill or talent. You are focusing upon your positive qualities.

"I'm _____". This variation is a bit more challenging. Using this variation, you just state the positive quality, such as "I'm coordinated" or "I'm rhythmic" or " I have a good memory". Most people find this more difficult to do. It may feel like you are boasting or bragging. However, taking time to appreciate your good qualities is neither boasting nor bragging. It is simply validating or appreciating yourself.

The Enhancing Quality Technique can also be done using two columns. In the first column you identify a time, place or a way you've experience a particular positive quality. In the second column you identify the actual quality. Prior to using this specific technique, you first identify some activities you enjoy doing and the strength, skill or talent you use to do them. Pick a specific positive quality you have and identify all the times, places or ways you have use it. Then identify the actual quality.

Time, Place or Way you've experienced this quality	Actual Quality

All of these techniques are designed to promote a solid sense of self esteem. If there's a particular quality you have that you feel is weak, you can strengthen it by using these techniques. Even if you feel you are lacking that particular quality, you can begin to identify ways that you actually have that quality – even though it may feel very weak to you. With practice, you can strengthen any positive quality.

Enhancing positive qualities is a way of strengthening those qualities you feel are weak or even those that you think (assume) that you don't have. By doing the Special Role Play you probably have identified some of those qualities. You also may have ASSUMMED that you didn't have such qualities. Now you know how you can strengthen them.

Ch 12 The Power of Assumptions

Assumptions are things we think or believe to be true, but we don't know if they are true. They can greatly influence your life. Consider the following goals:

1. starting your own business
2. finding a mate
3. losing weight or getting in shape
4. getting organized
5. become a better listener
6. going back to school
7. learning how to invest
8. writing a book
9. learning to play an instrument
10. joining a new club or activity group

Do you have any of the above goals? Are there personal changes that you would like to make in your life? Most likely, you have assumptions about them and oftentimes those assumptions are limiting or negative.

If you take any goal or anything you want to do but don't do it, chances are you have some negative or limiting assumptions about it. While anything that you want to do requires a plan and usually some knowledge or skills, they can be thwarted by a negative assumption. The assumption usually is something like, "I can't do that".

For example, suppose you want to lose some weight. You may be assuming that you can't lose weight or won't be successful in losing weight and keeping it off. You might be assuming something like, "I've always been overweight and that's the way I'm going to be"

Another possible assumption is, "I've tried so many diets and weight loss programs and none of them have worked. This one won't work either.

The problem with assuming anything is you just don't know if what you are assuming is true or not. Most of us allow assumptions to run our lives, often never questioning them or even aware that we are making assumptions. If you've been wanting to accomplish something and just haven't been able to even get started or have started but keep failing, chances are you have some assumptions about what you are attempting to do. Those assumptions are most likely limiting or negative.

The first step is to become aware that you are assuming – that you are making an assumption. The second step is to challenge the assumption. There are several ways of doing this. Some assumptions can easily be proven to be true or false by simply gathering some information. For example, if you assume that two quarts of liquid will fit into a gallon container, this is something that you can easily prove.

However, some assumptions are more difficult to prove. Oftentimes, personal assumptions or assumptions you are making about yourself require more scrutiny. Sometimes you can test your assumption to see if it is valid or not. Professor Robert Kegan of Harvard University has created an entire program called, "Unlocking the Immunity to Change", where he has people identify their "Big Assumption" and construct some simple tests to see if it is really true.

118

In this book, you have read about some critical thinking skills to determine if your assumptions are true or not. There is a process that I have developed to help you do this which I call the Special Role Play.

The phrase "critical thinking" can be somewhat confusing. Fortunately, for the purposes of "challenging" your assumptions, determining whether they are true or not, you can avoid getting bogged down in theoretical discussions of what critical thinking is and the formal names of various thinking skills. I've told you the names anyway, just for your own reference. However, this book emphasizes a practical approach – one that I have personally used with astounding results.

The first step is to identify assumptions – yours and assumptions made by other people. You can find them quite easily. Just remember that an assumption is something we take for granted. We think or believe it is true, but we don't really know if it is true. So, the next time you think of something, ask yourself, "Is this true?" "Is this an established fact?" If you can't answer "yes", then most likely, it is an assumption. Thinking something is true is not the same as <u>knowing</u> something is true.

You may have already made some assumptions about this book. Take a moment to identify some of them now.

- Did you assume that this book would be difficult to understand?
- What did you assume about this book? When you saw the title, what did you think? Was that an assumption?

It should be noted that not all assumptions are negative or restricting. However, the problem with assuming anything is that we simply don't know if the assumption is true or not. If it proves to be false, it could be embarrassing or even costly. Even worse, with personal assumptions, we are often unaware that we are being influenced by them. It is tragic that some people live their entire lives based upon an assumption that isn't true – and even worse, they are not even aware that that are doing so!

Therefore, it is important to be aware of your assumptions. While personal assumptions are much more sneaky to discover, they too can be discovered and challenged. If you find yourself saying "I can't", chances are you are making an assumption. Simply think about something you want to do, but haven't done it yet. Maybe it's something you've been wanting to do for years. If you find yourself saying, "I can't", you probably are assuming something.

Oftentimes when you start identifying personal assumptions, you will discover other assumptions associated with whatever assumption you have initially identified. It really doesn't matter where you begin because all personal assumptions can be challenged by using the Special Role Play and any qualities you have that you feel are weak or even lacking can be enhanced.

Assumptions can be very powerful. Some people run their entire lives based upon assumptions. They can control what you think, say or do. Usually people are unaware of their personal assumptions because they are hidden. However, they are easy to spot because personal assumptions are usually negative or restrictive. It's worth repeating - if you find yourself saying, "I can't", chances are you are making an assumption – something that is negative or restricts you in some way. People often experience a new found sense of personal freedom once they have identified their personal assumption and challenge it by using the Special Role Play.

When I first used this Process, I was amazed at the possibilities I discovered. It was like opening a door that I never even knew existed and finding all sorts of possibilities. I discovered potentials I never even knew existed. In a very real sense, the Special Role Play is very freeing and is how you challenge an assumption. The potential for you to change and improve the quality of your life exists and is available.

Assumptions are very powerful. They need to be challenged. They way you challenge them is to do the Special Role Play. After that, you can enhance any of the qualities you want that you feel are weak by using the enhancement techniques. If you haven't yet done the Special Role Play, what are you waiting for? It's like learning wilderness survival skills. You can read about it and watch videos. But you have to actually go out in the wilderness and do it. Just reading about it isn't enough. So, go do it NOW! Identify your personal assumptions, challenge them using the Special Role Play and then use some of the enhancement techniques. Let me know how you do.

Bob Schoenberg

APPENDICES

Appendix A – Frame of Reference Model

Appendix B – Satisfaction Quiz

Appendix C – Modified Mini Workshop

Appendix A

Frame of Reference Model

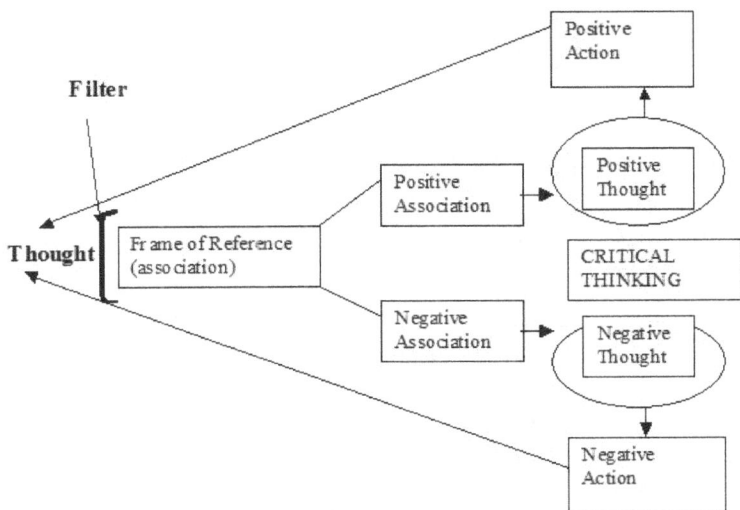

Frame of Reference Model Explanation

When you have a thought, it goes through a FILTER. The filter is a Frame of Reference or an association. That association will either be positive or negative depending upon what your experience was.

The Positive Mode

If your experience was positive your thought will be positive and you will take positive action.

The Negative Mode

If your experience was negative your thought will be negative, resulting in negative action.

Feedback Cycle

There is a feedback cycle whether the action is positive or negative. Each action results in a new thought starts the process to begin again.

Implications

A frame of reference can become an assumption and that assumption can be either negative or positive. Even a positive frame of reference can create an assumption and that assumption may be untrue. While we have been working primarily with personal assumptions, which tend to be negative, even a positive assumption needs to be checked out or at the very least, you need to be aware that you are making an assumption.

An example would be someone who goes to a particular service station for their car. They have a very good experience. As a result, the next time they need their car serviced, they return to the same service station thinking that since the last time was good, this time will also be good. (This is essentially a positive frame of reference that has become an assumption). But, things can change. Mechanics come and go. Some jobs are more difficult than others. Sometimes the management changes. Sometimes even the owner of the shop changes. But frequently, we base our opinion of a business on our frame of reference, which can become an assumption.

Appendix B

Find Your Personal Assumptions

Satisfaction Quiz

1. How satisfied are you with your professor/career

2. How satisfied are you with your weight?

3. How satisfied are you with your personal relationship

4. How satisfied are you with your social life/friendships

5. How satisfied are you with your health?

6. How satisfied are you with your financial life?

7. How satisfied are you with your living space?

What would you really like to do?

What is your ideal weight?

What type of relationship would you like?

What would your ideal social life be like?

What would your ideal health be like?

What would your ideal financial life be like

What would your ideal living space be like?

What would your idea spiritual life be like?

Choose one of the above that is really important to you. Identify what you think stops you from achieving it?

Ex. I want to run my own business. I can't because:

- I need capital and I can't get it.
- I'm no good at selling.
- I'm not smart enough to run my own business
- I'm too young/old to start my own business.
- I would fail at running my own business.

ALL of the above are ASSUMPTIONS!. Take one and challenge it!

Personal assumptions are negative or restrictive in nature and usually can be reduced to the phrase, "I can't … . While such personal assumptions are often hidden, they can be easily exposed. As soon as you find yourself saying "I can't", you have exposed one of your personal assumptions – unless you have actually proven the statement to be true.

Remember that personal assumptions can be sneaky. They might seem like they are really true. For example, I'm always going to be overweight because I've tried numerous diets and weight control programs and none of them worked. There are two assumptions here. One is that I'm always going to be overweight. The other assumption is "none of the diet or weight control programs work". This is an assumption, unless you have tried every single diet or weight control program. By the way, diets, don't work, but some weight control programs do.- especially those that teach you how to change your eating habits.

Oftentimes a group of assumptions will be linked together and support each other. It really doesn't matter where you begin to challenge your assumptions or which one you choose to tackle first. The important thing is to CHALLENGE them.

As you become more skilled, you will be able to easily recognize your personal assumptions and will be able to challenge them using the Special Role Play. Recall that the Special Role Play needs to be practiced. The more you use it the more skilled you will become as challenging your assumptions.

Remember there is a difference between personal assumptions and general assumptions. The later can usually be proven true or false merely by doing some research.

If you haven't already done so, take the quiz listed above and begin identifying your assumptions. Then pick one to challenge and use the Special Role Play to challenge it.

Appendix C

Modified Mini Workshop

The following are the essential skills that would be covered in an actual workshop. Of course, during a real workshop, you would participate in experiential exercises and have the benefit of a discussion and sharing of ideas.

Define what the word "assumption" means.

_____

There are two types of assumptions :

_____ and _____.

Provide an example of the first type of assumption you listed.

_____

Provide an example of the second type of assumption you listed.

_____

Explain how to do the Special Role Play.

_____

Choose a personal assumption. Identify it.

_____

Now, using the Special Role Play, what would a person who was the exact opposite of this think, say or do.

They would think the following:

_____

_____

_____

They would say the following:

_____

_____

_____

They would do the following:

_____

_____

_____

Make a list of all the positive qualities or skills or talents you've discovered.

1)

2)

3)

4)

5)

6)

7)

8)

9)

10)

If you have more than 10 use a blank piece of paper. Having more than 10 is fine.

For any of these skills, strengths or talents that you already have, place a check mark before each one. For those that you feel you have but are weak, place a question mark before each one. For those you feel you just don't have, place an X before each one.

Your next task is to use the Enhancement Techniques for any items you placed question mark or an X. Choose one item that you have labeled with a question mark. Take that quality and identify all the times, places or ways you have used that technique. For example, let's say you chose the quality of "being organized". You would identify all the various ways that you are organized. (Before you say, "but I'm unorganized", everyone has some sort of organization to what they do - even if it isn't the most efficient way of doing something). Here are some hints: where do you keep your dishes? Do you stack them in any particular order or are your dishes mixed up with cups and saucers and other items. You probably have them stacked by category or by usage. How about your clothing. Do you put them in a closet or have them literally all over the house – even on the floor. (I've actually seen this). What about clothes that need to be washed? Do you store them in one area, such as a clothes basket or hamper?

Get the idea? You do have some sort of organization. Now continue to identify other ways that you are organized.

Using other techniques, continue to develop your organizational skills. You can use any of the following: "I like how I'm _____" or "I'm _____". Do this for each quality you feel you are lacking or for any that feel inferior.

Bibliography

Elbow, Peter. 1973. <u>Writing Without Teachers</u>. NY. Oxford University Press 1986.

"Methodological Doubt and Believing Contraries in Inquiry", <u>Embracing Contraries</u>. NY. Oxford University Press.

_____.2009. .Journal of the Assembly for Expanded Perspectives on Learning.

Kegan, Robert. 2015. "Immunity to Change". Massive Open Online Course (MOOC), EDX. Harvard University.

Losier, J. Micheal. 2009. <u>Law of Attraction</u>. Michael J. Losier. Victoria, BC, Canada

Malkasian, Daniela.. 2014. Unpublished Paper, "Assumptions and Frames of Reference in a Legally Blind Student". Final Project. Graduate Critical Thinking Class. University o fMassachusetts at Boston. Fall semester.

Paul, Richard. 1990. Critical Thinking. Rohnert Park: Sonoma State University.

Nagle, R.J. and G. Smith. 1995. "Frames of Reference and Buyer's Perception of Price and Value". <u>California Management Review</u>. Fall.

Sargent. Thomas. 1984.. <u>The Behavioral and Medical Effects of Stress.</u> Hartford, CT Designed Change Institue Publications.

Schoenberg. Bob. <u>Designed Change Process</u>. 2013. Science and Humanities Press. Saint Charles, MO USA

_____. Critical Thinking in Business 2nd Edition. 2015. Science and Humanities Press. Saint Charles, MO USA

About the Author

Bob Schoenberg, M.A. is a Professor of Critical & Creative Thinking. For 12 years he taught an online graduate course in *Critical Thinking* which he created for the University of Massachusetts at Boston. He also created and taught another graduate course entitled, *Critical Thinking in Business*, modeled after his book by the same title. Prior to teaching online, Mr. Schoenberg taught regular face to face courses in Critical Thinking at MassBay Community College and served as a Training Specialist to various businesses and organizations.

Mr. Schoenberg was a guest speaker at the Critical Thinking Conference held at the Community College of RI (Warwick Campus) and has been a frequent presenter at the annual Technology Conferences at the University of Massachusetts at Boston. He is the author of three other books published by Science and Humanities

In this book, <u>Stop Assuming</u>, Bob has stepped out of academia and written a book in an easy to understand, user friendly style that focuses upon practical skills and techniques which are based upon a solid framework of critical thinking. Yet, throughout the entire book, he rarely mentions that term and avoids using jargon . Instead, he offers simple and easy to understand information and instructions that enable the reader to Stop Assuming. Unlike most authors, he puts all the nuts and bolts at the beginning of the book and doesn't require you to wade through numerous chapters to get the good stuff. In addition, Bob even gives you his email address and encourages you to email him if you have questions or comments – a rarity for most authors.

In addition to conducting workshops in southeastern Massachusetts and Rhode Island, Bob also offers classes online at this website STOP ASSUMING.org. He can be reached at Info@StopAssuming.org.

Other Books by Bob Schoenberg

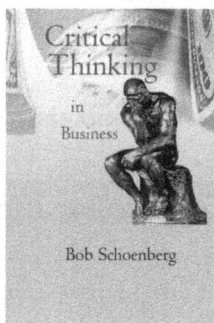

An MBA is not enough.

While there are a number of business schools that recognize the importance of critical thinking, few, if any, offer a specific course in critical thinking. Faculty members are experts in their respective fields: accounting, finance, management, marketing, sales, etc. But critical thinking, although interdisciplinary, is not specifically a business skill. Yet, successful business people do use critical thinking.

In this book, Bob Schoenberg, a recognized teacher and consultant on critical thinking skills, outlines key tools and attitudes to help think more effectively about common business issues.

From assumptions to frames of reference to ethics, critical thinking is the key to more effective business decisions.

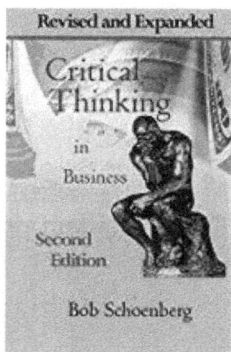

In the Revised and Expanded Second Edition

Added more exercises, an appendix, a new chapter on critical thinking and social media and other materials.

Designed Change Process

Managing Stress, Feelings and Behavior

Bob Schoenberg

Change for Success:

The Designed Change Process, (D.C.P.) offers people an opportunity to make positive changes in their lives by increasing their sense of self esteem, managing feelings (stress) and changing unwanted behavior patterns. Whether you are stuck in a pattern, bombarded by stress or want to enhance your sense of self esteem, the D.C.P. will provide you with the tools to change for success. In this book, Bob Schoenberg, a recognized teacher and consultant in critical thinking skills and an expert in the Designed Change Process, provides techniques and skills to help you apply the Designed Change Process. From ways of managing feelings to self esteem enhancement to changing behavior patterns, the Designed Change Process provides you with specific information and skills and make positive changes in your life.

All are available at **Science and Humanities Press** or via **Amazon.com**.